PRAYING THROUGH THE NAMES OF GOD

THE SUPREME G☨D

Books 5–8 • Collected Edition

EL SHADDAI • EL OLAM
EL ROI • EL GIBBOR

Prayers to Experience God's Power, Presence and Care

CYRIL OPOKU

The Supreme God: *Prayers to Experience God's Power, Presence and Care (Collected Edition: Books 5 to 8)*

© 2025 Cyril Opoku. *PrayerScripts*. All rights reserved.

No part of this publication may be reproduced, stored in a retrieval system, or transmitted in any form or by any means—electronic, mechanical, photocopy, recording, or otherwise—without the prior written permission of the publisher, except in the case of brief quotations used in reviews, articles, or devotionals.

Published by *Quest Publications (questpublications@outlook.com)*

ISBN: 978-1-988439-99-0

Unless otherwise indicated, all Scripture quotations are taken from the World English Bible WEB, which is in the public domain. For more information, visit: www.worldenglish.bible

This book is a work of devotional encouragement. It is not intended to replace biblical study, pastoral counsel, or professional therapy.

Printed in the United States of America.

First Edition: December 2025

For more books like this, visit *PrayerScripts:* https://prayerscripts.org

Contents

Contents iii
Preface viii
Introduction x
How to Use PrayerScripts xii

Preface to Book 5 2
Introduction to Book 5 4
1. Majesty in Covenant Power 5
2. Blessing from the Almighty 8
3. Increase Under the Almighty 11
4. Mercy from the Almighty 14
5. Blessings of the Almighty 17
6. Revealed as the Almighty 20
7. Strength in His Voice 22
8. Restored by the Almighty 24
9. Sustained Through Affliction 26
10. Pierced Yet Preserved by the Almighty 28
11. Restored by the Almighty's Justice 30
12. Unsearchable Greatness of the Almighty 33
13. Refined by the Almighty 35
14. Kept in the Knowledge of the Almighty 37
15. Breathed Upon by the Almighty 39
16. Shielded by the Almighty 41
17. Strengthened by the Almighty 43
18. Victory Under the Almighty's Voice 45
19. Daily Sustained by the Almighty 47
20. Dwelling Under the Almighty's Shadow 49
21. Renewed by Almighty Strength 51
22. Nourished by the Almighty 53
23. Awed by the Almighty's Voice 55

24. Stirred by the Almighty's Movement 57
25. Roaring Deliverance of the Almighty 59
26. All Things Possible with the Almighty 61
27. Power Perfected Through the Almighty 63
28. Abundantly Supplied by the Almighty 65
29. Saved Completely by the Almighty 67
30. The Eternal Almighty 69

Preface to Book 6 72
Introduction to Book 6 74
31. Enduring Strength Revealed 75
32. Everlasting Refuge 78
33. Unchanging Glory 81
34. Eternal Goodness Endures 84
35. Timeless Majesty 87
36. King Forever 90
37. Blessed Forever 93
38. Generations in His Hands 95
39. Established Forever 98
40. Forever Faithful 101
41. Unchanging Through All Ages 103
42. Throne Established Forever 106
43. Mercy That Never Ends 109
44. Word Forever Settled 111
45. Eternity Placed Within 113
46. Rock of Ages 115
47. Strength Without Weariness 117
48. The God Who Declares the End 119
49. Majesty of Eternity 121
50. Everlasting Love 123

51. Reigning Forever 125
52. King of Heaven Forever 127
53. Ancient of Days, Unmoving 129
54. The Eternal God Revealed 131
55. Immortal Majesty 133
56. Eternal Spirit 135
57. Forever the Same 137
58. The Word That Lives Forever 139
59. The God Who Is, Was, and Is to Come 141
60. The Living One Forever 143

Preface to Book 7 146
Introduction to Book 7 148
61. The God Who Finds Me 149
62. Kept in His Watchful Presence 152
63. The God Who Remembers My Cry 155
64. Seen in My Affliction 158
65. Held as His Treasure 160
66. Strengthened Under His Eyes 162
67. Refined by His Seeing 165
68. Held in His Compassion 167
69. Kept Under His Eye 169
70. Rejoicing in His Seeing 171
71. Guided by His Instruction 173
72. Observed by Heaven 175
73. Rescued in His Nearness 177
74. My Tears in His Book 179
75. Surrounded by His Knowing 181
76. Seen in Every Path 184
77. Upheld by His Righteous Right Hand 186

v

78. Protected in the Waters and Fire 188
79. Engraved on His Hands 190
80. Known Before I Began 192
81. Watched with Intentional Goodness 194
82. Planted Under His Watchful Care 196
83. Seen, Heard, and Strengthened 198
84. Rewarded in the Secret Place 200
85. Numbered and Protected 202
86. Moved with Compassion Toward Me 204
87. Known by the Good Shepherd 206
88. Laid Bare Before His Eyes 208
89. Beholding His Eyes Upon Me 210
90. Known in Every Work 212

Preface to Book 8 216
Introduction to Book 8 218
91. Triumph Born of Majesty 219
92. The Warrior of My Salvation 221
93. Stand Still and See Victory 223
94. He Fights Before Me 225
95. The God Who Fights for Me 227
96. One Can Chase a Thousand 229
97. The Lord Is With You, Mighty Warrior 231
98. The God of My Deliverance 233
99. My Rock and Fortress 235
100. Rescued by His Power 237
101. The King of Glory in Battle 239
102. Fearless in the Face of Battle 241
103. Your Right Hand Has Saved Us 243
104. The Warrior Who Breaks Bows 245

105. The God Who Rules the Seas 247
106. Mountains Melt Before Him 249
107. Returning to the Mighty God 251
108. The Hero Who Marches Forth 253
109. The Lord Is With Me as a Mighty Warrior 255
110. Nothing Too Hard for the Mighty God 257
111. The Voice That Commands Armies 259
112. The Jealous Warrior Who Defends His People 261
113. The Warrior Who Rejoices Over Me 263
114. All Authority Belongs to the Mighty One 265
115. Overcoming Through the Mighty Christ 267
116. More Than Conquerors Through Him 269
117. Pulling Down Strongholds 271
118. Standing Strong in the Mighty Lord 273
119. Greater Is He Within Me 275
120. The Rider on the White Horse 277

Epilogue *281*
Encourage Others with Your Story *283*
More from PrayerScripts *284*

Preface

"Those who know your name will put their trust in you, for you, Yahweh, have not forsaken those who seek you."
— Psalms 9:10 (WEB)

This verse speaks to a trust that is no longer theoretical, but lived—tested in time, refined through seasons, and strengthened by experience. Psalm 9:10 declares that knowing God's Name produces confidence not because life is easy, but because God is faithful. This truth anchors this print volume compiling **Books 5–8 of *The Supreme God***—a sacred continuation of the journey into the Names of God that moves from foundational revelation into lived encounter.

These four books—**El Shaddai, El Olam, El Roi,** and **El Gibbor**—reveal how the Supreme God meets His people in the realities of life. Here, God is known not only as sovereign and exalted, but as sufficient in weakness, constant through time, attentive to the unseen, and mighty in battle. These Names speak directly to seasons where faith is stretched, endurance is required, and trust must be anchored in more than understanding alone.

This volume was created for the believer who has come to know who God is—and now needs to experience how that truth sustains, strengthens, and carries them forward. El Shaddai reveals the God who supplies what you cannot produce. El Olam anchors you in the God who remains when seasons change. El Roi assures you that nothing about your life is overlooked. El Gibbor proclaims that the God you trust is active, victorious, and strong on your behalf. Together, these Names form a testimony of God's nearness and power in the lived experience of faith.

As you enter this volume, you are not starting again—you are going deeper. You are learning to trust God not only for beginnings, but for endurance; not only for revelation, but for victory. The same God who revealed His identity in earlier pages now reveals His care, strength, and faithfulness in motion. He has not forsaken you. He is meeting you here—proving that those who know His Name can trust Him fully, even in the midst of life's demands.

To the Praise of His Name!
Cyril O.
(Illinois | December 2025)

Introduction

Faith matures when what you know about God begins to sustain how you live with Him.

This print volume compiling **Books 5–8 of *The Supreme God*** exists for that sacred transition— from knowing God's identity to experiencing His presence and power in everyday life. These four books form **Part 1B** of the series, carrying the reader beyond foundational revelation into lived trust. Here, God is encountered as the All-Sufficient One, the Everlasting God, the God Who Sees, and the Mighty Warrior—Names that speak directly into seasons of need, waiting, vulnerability, and spiritual conflict.

A defining feature throughout this volume is the *Devotional Insight* that accompanies every Scripture. These insights are intentionally placed to slow the reader's pace and prepare the heart before prayer. They help translate eternal truth into present awareness—highlighting where God is already sustaining, seeing, strengthening, and fighting on your behalf. Rather than rushing into words, the *Devotional Insight* invites reflection, recognition, and alignment, allowing prayer to rise from trust rather than strain.

The rhythm of Scripture, *Devotional Insight*, and *PrayerScript* is especially vital in this portion of the series. These books are not about abstract belief; they are about faith that holds steady in real life. The Devotional Insight becomes a bridge—connecting what Scripture declares with what the believer is experiencing, and guiding prayer from a place of confidence rather than desperation.

This volume is designed to be read slowly, prayed deeply, and returned to often. It also stands in relationship with the companion print collection featuring **Books 1-4**, which lays the foundational revelation of God's identity and authority. Readers who have not yet journeyed through those earlier books are warmly invited to explore them, as together both volumes form a complete and strengthening portrait of the Supreme God.

As you move through these pages, may trust deepen—not because circumstances change immediately, but because the God you know is proving Himself faithful in every season.

How to Use PrayerScripts

This book is designed as a daily companion to guide you into a prophetic lifestyle of prayer. This is a prayer journey meant to position you to walk in the fullness of God's promises. Here's how to make the most of it:

1. Dedicate a Daily Time:

Set aside a consistent time each day to engage with the prayer for that day. Treat this as sacred time with God, where distractions are minimized, and your heart is fully focused on communion with Him. Ten to twenty minutes daily is sufficient to meditate on the Scripture, pray, and receive revelation.

2. Begin with Scripture Reflection:

Each day begins with a carefully selected Scripture. Read it slowly, meditate on its meaning, and let the Holy Spirit illuminate how it applies to your life. Allow the Word to penetrate your spirit and prepare you to pray from a place of faith and expectancy.

3. Pray the Guided Prayer

Use the prayer provided as a framework, allowing it to resonate with your own words and personal circumstances. Speak each declaration with authority and confidence, fully believing that God is at work. You may also pause to personalize the prayer for your specific family, career, or ministry needs.

- *Make It Personal*

  These prayers are written in the first person so you can make them your own. Speak them aloud, inserting the names of your family members, your workplace, your church, or your city where applicable. The more you personalize the prayer, the more you will sense its power shaping your reality.

- *Pray with Authority*

  These are not timid requests; they are bold decrees. Lift your voice as a covenant child of God, covered by the blood of Jesus and backed by heaven's authority. When you pray, do so with confidence that Christ has already won the victory on your behalf.

- *Leave Room for the Holy Spirit*

  These written prayers are a guide, not a limit. As you pray, pause to listen. The Holy Spirit may give you prophetic words, insights, or specific instructions. Follow His lead. Allow Him to expand the prayer, add declarations, or guide you into deeper intercession.

4. *Journal Your Insights:*

Keep a notebook or journal to record any thoughts, revelations, or confirmations you receive during prayer. Writing down what God speaks to you helps solidify understanding and creates a record of breakthrough and growth over time.

5. *Repeat as Needed:*

Some prayers or themes may need to be revisited multiple times. Answer to prayer is progressive; the more you engage with these prayers in faith, the greater the manifestation in your life and household. You can return to this book at any season to reinforce your victory and dominion.

6. *Live in Expectancy:*

Prayer is only one part of walking in enlargement—your actions, faith, and obedience amplify the power of these prayers. Move boldly into opportunities, embrace the doors God opens, and live with a confident expectation that God is answering your prayer beyond what you can see or imagine.

By following this guide daily, you will cultivate a lifestyle of prayer and kingdom impact. Let this book be your companion as you step into the new dimensions God has destined for you.

The Supreme God

אֵל שַׁדַּי

EL SHADDAI
God Almighty

*Prayers to Draw Strength from
The All-Sufficient One*

CYRIL OPOKU

Preface to Book 5

"Those who know your name will put their trust in you, for you, Yahweh, have not forsaken those who seek you."

— Psalms 9:10 (WEB)

To know God's Name is to discover the place where trust is born and fear loses its hold. Psalm 9:10 reveals a sacred pattern: *those who know His Name learn to trust Him*, and those who trust Him discover that He never forsakes those who seek Him. This truth stands at the heart of **Book 5—EL SHADDAI: God Almighty**. El Shaddai is the God whose power is not distant or abstract, but deeply personal, sustaining, and sufficient for every need. He is the Almighty who nourishes, strengthens, protects, and supplies—never abandoning those who lean fully upon Him.

Throughout Scripture, El Shaddai reveals Himself as the God who meets people at the limits of their strength. When human ability ends, His sufficiency begins. He is not merely strong; He is *more than enough*. He is the God who supports the weary, carries the weak, and faithfully provides when resources fail and hope feels thin. To know Him by this Name is to learn that your trust is not misplaced, your seeking is not wasted, and your dependence is not a liability—it is an invitation for divine strength to manifest.

As you enter this book, allow your heart to rest in the assurance that El Shaddai is not intimidated by your need. He is drawn to it. Every prayer within these pages is designed to help you shift from self-reliance to God-reliance, from anxiety to confidence, and from striving to rest. May this book deepen your trust, enlarge your faith, and anchor your soul in the God who has never forsaken—and never will forsake—those who seek Him.

To the Praise of His Name!
Cyril O.
(Illinois | December 2025)

Introduction to Book 5

Every believer eventually discovers that strength has limits—but God does not.

EL SHADDAI—*God Almighty* invites you into the liberating revelation that you do not have to be enough, because God already is. This fifth book in *The Supreme God* series focuses on God's all-sufficient power—His ability to sustain, provide, strengthen, and uphold you in every season of life. El Shaddai is the God you lean on when life feels heavy, when responsibilities stretch you thin, and when the future feels uncertain. He is the Almighty who does not merely command power but releases it tenderly into the lives of those who trust Him.

As part of **Part 1 (Books 1–8)** of the series, this book builds upon the revelations of Elohim (Creator), Yahweh (Eternal I AM), Adonai (Lord and Master), and El Elyon (God Most High). You are encouraged to continue exploring the remaining Names in Part 1—El Olam, El Roi, and El Gibbor—before advancing into **Part 2 (Books 9–16)**, where God's glory, truth, knowledge, holiness, life, heavenly authority, and kingship unfold in greater depth.

This book is an invitation to trust deeply, rest fully, and rely confidently on El Shaddai—the God who is more than enough for everything you will ever face.

1

Majesty in Covenant Power

> "When Abram was ninety-nine years old, Yahweh appeared to Abram and said to him, 'I am God Almighty. Walk before me and be blameless. I will make my covenant between me and you, and will multiply you exceedingly.'"
> — Genesis 17:1–2 WEB

Devotional Insight

El Shaddai reveals Himself to Abram not simply as a powerful deity but as the God who is enough—strong enough to perform what He promises and tender enough to uphold the frailty of His servant. In this moment, Abram learns that divine sufficiency is the anchor of covenant living. God Almighty sustains, multiplies, empowers, and transforms. For the believer today, El Shaddai remains the Mighty One who supplies strength when our natural capacity collapses. He invites us to walk before Him with confidence, not because we are flawless, but because He is faithful. When God declares Himself as El Shaddai, He unveils His ability to bring forth what seems impossible, to nourish our faith, and to multiply His purposes in our lives.

His sufficiency becomes our strength; His covenant becomes our security.

Prayer

O El Shaddai, God Almighty, I stand before You in awe of Your covenant strength and overflowing sufficiency. You are the God who steps into impossibility and declares that nothing is too hard for You. Today I lift my heart before Your majesty and ask that You shape my walk to reflect the glory of Your Name. Let every place of insufficiency in me be overshadowed by Your endless might.

El Shaddai, breathe upon my journey. Where I have felt weak, weary, or stretched beyond what I can bear, be my nourishing strength. Pour Your sustaining power into the hidden places of my life. Make me upright before You—not by my own striving but by Your divine enablement. Cause my life to flourish in alignment with Your covenant promises.

God Almighty, multiply what seems small in my hands. Multiply grace in my character, increase fruitfulness in my calling, and expand wisdom in my decisions. Where barrenness has lingered, release supernatural productivity. Where delay has discouraged me, awaken fresh faith. Where doubt has whispered, silence every voice that contradicts Your Word.

El Shaddai, let Your sufficiency become the atmosphere of my home and family. Strengthen the weary, nourish the discouraged, and lift the broken. Let Your covenant promises operate in every generation connected to me. Establish divine stability where instability has threatened to rule.

I yield fully to Your omnipotent hand. Walk with me, shape me, and display Your might through me. Let my life testify that El Shaddai is still faithful, still powerful, and still performing His Word. In Jesus' name, Amen.

2

Blessing from the Almighty

"May God Almighty bless you, and make you fruitful, and multiply you, that you may be a company of peoples."
— Genesis 28:3 WEB

Devotional Insight

El Shaddai is the God who blesses with fruitfulness, expansion, and divine empowerment. When Isaac speaks these words over Jacob, he invokes the sufficiency and might of God to carry Jacob into a future he cannot shape on his own. El Shaddai is the One who takes small beginnings and turns them into nations, who breathes increase where there has been lack, and who ensures that His purposes unfold beyond human ability. For believers today, this Name assures us that God's blessing is more than a pleasant wish—it is divine enablement that produces supernatural outcomes. El Shaddai enlarges capacity, strengthens identity, and fuels destiny. His blessing empowers us to grow, flourish, and multiply in the spheres He appoints for us. We trust Him because His sufficiency is limitless and His intentions toward us overflow with life.

Prayer

El Shaddai, God Almighty, I receive the blessing of Your sufficiency over my life today. You are the God who multiplies, the God who increases, the God who transforms small seeds into abundant harvests. I stand before You in expectation, knowing that Your blessing does not merely touch my circumstances—it reshapes my destiny.

God Almighty, breathe fruitfulness into every area where You have planted me. Let the work of my hands prosper under Your power. Let my family flourish under Your covering. Let the gifts and assignments You have entrusted to me multiply with supernatural momentum. Where there has been stagnation, release acceleration. Where there has been emptiness, release overflow.

El Shaddai, stretch my capacity. Expand my spiritual understanding, deepen my faith, enlarge my influence for Your glory. Make me a vessel through whom many are blessed. Let the increase You release into my life become a testimony of Your unfailing power and kindness.

Father, I pray that Your mighty blessing will saturate every generation connected to me. Establish a legacy rooted in Your faithfulness. Let doors open that no man can shut. Let opportunities arise that only Your hand could orchestrate. Surround my path with divine favor and secure every step in Your ordained will.

God Almighty, I yield my plans to Your perfect purposes. Multiply what I could never produce on my own. Shape my life into a living witness that El Shaddai still blesses abundantly. In Jesus' name, Amen.

3

Increase Under the Almighty

"God said to him, 'I am God Almighty. Be fruitful and multiply. A nation and a company of nations will be from you, and kings will come out of your body.'"
— Genesis 35:11 WEB

Devotional Insight

El Shaddai speaks destiny-defining words over Jacob, revealing Himself as the One whose sufficiency births nations, identities, and futures far beyond human reach. God Almighty does not merely promise growth—He commands it, empowers it, and sustains it. As El Shaddai, He imparts strength for generational transformation and establishes identity rooted in divine purpose. For believers today, this Name reminds us that our increase, influence, and spiritual fruitfulness are not self-produced; they are God-enabled. El Shaddai calls forth what He has already ordained, expands what seems limited, and shapes outcomes that reveal His glory. When God Almighty speaks increase, nothing in the natural can hinder His design. We move forward not by human striving but by divine empowerment.

Prayer

El Shaddai, God Almighty, I bow before Your majesty and receive the decree of increase You speak over my life. You are the God who calls nations out of individuals and brings generational purpose out of those who feel unqualified. Today I stand under the weight of Your glory and the beauty of Your sufficiency.

El Shaddai, activate every divine assignment buried within me. Let dormant gifts awaken, let hidden strengths rise, let untapped grace emerge with clarity and power. Release the spiritual fruitfulness that only Your hand can produce. Increase my capacity to serve, to lead, to love, and to influence according to Your will.

God Almighty, let generational blessings flow through my lineage. Establish kingship, leadership, spiritual authority, and kingdom identity in my family. Break every limitation that has lingered over past generations and usher in a new lineage marked by divine strength and covenant favor.

El Shaddai, nurture every seed You have planted in my life. Guard it from fear, doubt, delay, and opposition. Let Your power overshadow every weakness. Transform my insufficiency into testimonies of Your might. Cause Your promises to manifest in ways that exceed my imagination.

Father, I yield my future to the hand of the Almighty. Guide my steps into the fullness of what You ordained long before

I was formed. Let my life, my legacy, and my lineage display the greatness of El Shaddai. In Jesus' name, Amen.

4

Mercy from the Almighty

"May God Almighty give you mercy before the man, that he may release to you your other brother and Benjamin. If I am bereaved of my children, I am bereaved."
— Genesis 43:14 WEB

Devotional Insight

In a moment of deep uncertainty, Jacob invokes El Shaddai as the God whose sufficiency includes mercy, intervention, and compassionate oversight. El Shaddai is not only powerful—He is tender, near, and attentive to the cries of His people. Jacob entrusts his family to the Almighty, acknowledging that the outcome rests in God's hands alone. For the believer today, El Shaddai remains the God who goes before us into difficult places, who softens hearts, who orchestrates favor, and who releases mercy where judgment or loss once seemed inevitable. His sufficiency covers our fears, our vulnerabilities, and the places we cannot control. We learn that trust in El Shaddai is not passive resignation—it is active surrender to the One who holds every outcome in His omnipotent love.

Prayer

El Shaddai, God Almighty, I come to You in full surrender, trusting that Your mercy is powerful enough to overturn every fearful expectation. You are the God who intervenes with compassion, who goes ahead of me into places I cannot enter, and who orchestrates outcomes beyond my reach.

God Almighty, release mercy over every situation that concerns me. Let Your tender strength touch relationships strained by misunderstanding or distance. Let mercy rewrite stories where loss once seemed certain. Let Your compassion speak where my voice cannot reach. Go before me and prepare the hearts of those whose decisions impact my life and the lives of those I love.

El Shaddai, cover my family under the shelter of Your sufficiency. Where fear has gripped us, release peace. Where anxiety has tried to rule, release assurance. Where relationships have fractured, release reconciliation by Your mighty hand. Surround us with Your mercy like a shield.

Lord, I place every vulnerable place in Your hands—every fear for the future, every uncertainty, every burden that tries to weigh me down. You are sufficient. You are mighty. You are merciful. Let Your intervention manifest in supernatural ways, turning hearts, opening doors, and restoring what seemed lost.

El Shaddai, strengthen my trust. Teach me to rest in the assurance that You hold every outcome and that Your mercy never fails. Let my life become a testimony that God

Almighty still moves with compassion and power. In Jesus' name, Amen.

5

Blessings of the Almighty

"Even by the God of your father, who will help you, by the Almighty, who will bless you with blessings of heaven above, blessings of the deep that lies beneath, blessings of the breasts, and of the womb. The blessings of your father have prevailed above the blessings of my ancestors to the utmost bound of the everlasting hills."
— Genesis 49:25–26 WEB

Devotional Insight

In Jacob's final prophetic blessing, El Shaddai is revealed as the God whose sufficiency pours out blessings from every realm—heavenly, earthly, physical, and generational. God Almighty is not limited to one dimension of provision; His blessings overflow into every area of need and promise. For the believer, El Shaddai remains the One who helps, sustains, nourishes, and releases generational abundance. His sufficiency reaches into the deepest parts of our lives— our identity, our purpose, our family lines, and even the hidden places where only His Spirit can work. El Shaddai's blessing prevails because it originates from His eternal might and compassionate care. When He blesses, no earthly circumstance can diminish the outcome. His sufficiency is total, tender, and triumphant.

Prayer

El Shaddai, God Almighty, I stand beneath the waterfall of Your blessings and open my heart to receive the fullness of Your sufficiency. You are the God who helps, the God who sustains, the God who releases abundance from realms visible and invisible. Today I declare that my life is covered by the blessing of the Almighty.

God Almighty, pour out heavenly blessings upon my spirit—wisdom, revelation, discernment, purity, and the joy of Your presence. Let the deep wells beneath my life spring forth with strength, stability, and resilience. Let physical blessings—health, vitality, nourishment, and restoration—flow from Your sufficiency.

El Shaddai, bless my family with generational strength. Release blessings that outlive me, blessings that outlast adversity, blessings that shape the destinies of my children and their children. Let the hills of generational adversity crumble under the weight of Your prevailing favor.

God Almighty, bless the work of my hands, the dreams of my heart, and the assignments You have entrusted to me. Let nothing remain barren that You have chosen to bring to life. Let every area of need be met by Your limitless sufficiency.

El Shaddai, I rest in the certainty that when You bless, no opposition can diminish it and no circumstance can steal it.

Let my life testify that the blessings of the Almighty still prevail with unstoppable power and tender care. In Jesus' name, Amen.

6

Revealed as the Almighty

"I appeared to Abraham, to Isaac, and to Jacob, as God Almighty; but by my name Yahweh I was not known to them."
— Exodus 6:3 WEB

Devotional Insight

El Shaddai is the Name by which God revealed His sufficiency and strength to the patriarchs. Before Israel knew Him as Yahweh—the covenant-keeping God—they experienced Him as El Shaddai, the One who sustains and empowers beyond human ability. This revelation teaches that God meets His people with the aspect of His nature they need most in their season. El Shaddai carries, upholds, and nourishes the believer with divine strength. He is the God who shows Himself mighty on behalf of His people long before they fully understand His ways. Today, believers still encounter Him as the all-sufficient One who undergirds weakness and proves Himself faithful through every generation. El Shaddai is the One who stands unchanged, unwavering, and eternally enough.

Prayer

El Shaddai, God Almighty, I worship You as the One who reveals Yourself according to my need and You who sustain me with tender strength. I thank You that before I ever knew the fullness of Your covenant ways, You were already carrying me, providing for me, and fighting for me. You are the God of Abraham, Isaac, and Jacob, and You remain the same in my life today.

God Almighty, show Yourself strong in the areas where I feel weak or uncertain. Let Your sufficiency overshadow every insufficiency within me. Lift me above the anxieties that seek to distract me from Your faithfulness. Reveal Your sustaining presence in every circumstance—whether joyful or challenging.

El Shaddai, nourish my faith with fresh strength. Let Your power fortify my spirit, granting me the endurance to walk confidently in Your promises. Remind me that You have not changed, and the same God who upheld the patriarchs also upholds me.

Lord, reveal more of Your nature to me as I walk with You. Let every step I take be anchored in the truth that You are enough—more than enough—to accomplish all You have promised. Strengthen my family with the revelation of Your sufficiency. Let each one experience Your might and mercy personally.

May my life reflect deep trust in El Shaddai, the God who is eternally faithful and infinitely strong. In Jesus' name, Amen.

7

Strength in His Voice

"He says, who hears the words of God, who sees the vision of the Almighty, falling down, and having his eyes open: how goodly are your tents, Jacob, and your tents, Israel!"
— Numbers 24:4–6 WEB

Devotional Insight

El Shaddai opens eyes that were once closed and reveals beauty where others see nothing but wilderness. In this prophetic moment, the Almighty allows Balaam to perceive what only God's perspective can reveal—Israel blessed, ordered, flourishing under divine oversight. El Shaddai enables believers to see beyond natural circumstances into the reality of God's intention. Today, the Almighty still grants His people spiritual sight, clarity, and understanding. He opens eyes to identity, purpose, and destiny. He reveals beauty, provision, and blessing that the natural mind may overlook. To walk with El Shaddai is to see life through the lens of divine sufficiency and supernatural revelation.

Prayer

El Shaddai, God Almighty, open my eyes to behold what You see. Let me hear Your words with clarity and perceive Your works with unveiled vision. You are the God who reveals beauty in unlikely places and blessing where others see barrenness. Today I ask for fresh sight—sight shaped by Your might, not my limitations.

God Almighty, let Your revelation break through every place of confusion. Where my vision has been clouded by fear, doubt, or distraction, let Your voice bring clarity. Teach me to see my life, my family, and my destiny from Your vantage point. Reveal the tents of blessing You've set around me—Your covering, Your protection, Your goodness.

El Shaddai, open my spiritual eyes so I may discern opportunities You have ordained and dangers You have shielded me from. Let me recognize the beauty of Your order and the richness of Your provision. Show me the paths of blessing hidden within ordinary moments.

Lord, let Your revelation strengthen my confidence in Your plan. Root me deeply in the assurance that I am surrounded by Your sufficiency. Let my household flourish under Your oversight. Let my children and every generation connected to me dwell in the beauty and order of Your divine arrangement.

El Shaddai, speak continually to my heart. Let every word You reveal nourish me with strength and hope. Lead me by revelation, shape me by Your voice, and transform me by Your vision. In Jesus' name, Amen.

8

Restored by the Almighty

> "She said to them, 'Don't call me Naomi. Call me Mara, for the Almighty has dealt very bitterly with me. I went out full, and Yahweh has brought me home again empty. Why do you call me Naomi, since Yahweh has testified against me, and the Almighty has afflicted me?'"
> — Ruth 1:20–21 WEB

Devotional Insight

Naomi speaks from a place of grief, yet even in her lament she acknowledges God as El Shaddai—the One whose sovereignty governs every season. She perceives loss, but what she cannot yet see is restoration already forming under the Almighty's hand. El Shaddai is the God who meets us in sorrow but refuses to leave us in emptiness. He is sufficient in seasons of fullness and seasons of famine. He is working redemptively even when we cannot trace His hand. For the believer, this passage reminds us that God Almighty is both powerful and tender—strong enough to rebuild what was lost and merciful enough to heal what was broken. Our emptiness becomes the canvas upon which His sufficiency is revealed.

Prayer

El Shaddai, God Almighty, I bring before You every place in my heart that feels empty, wounded, or weary. You are the God who sees me in seasons of loss, yet You are also the God who restores beyond imagination. I surrender my pain into Your hands, trusting that Your sovereignty is never separated from Your compassion.

God Almighty, breathe life into the places that feel barren. Let Your sufficiency swallow every sense of lack. Where disappointment has lingered, release healing. Where bitterness has tried to take root, cleanse my heart with Your mercy. Let the story You are writing move me from Mara to Naomi again—from bitterness to pleasantness, from emptiness to fullness.

El Shaddai, rebuild what was torn down in my life. Restore relationships, opportunities, joy, and identity. Let Your redemptive plan unfold in ways I cannot yet perceive. Surround my family with hope that springs from Your sufficiency alone.

Lord, let Your presence rewrite my narrative. Turn sorrow into strength and loss into legacy. Help me to trust that even when I cannot trace Your hand, Your heart toward me is good. You are the Almighty who transforms ashes into beauty and mourning into dancing.

El Shaddai, carry me through every season with Your tender might. Let my restoration glorify Your Name. In Jesus' name, Amen.

9

Sustained Through Affliction

"Behold, happy is the man whom God corrects. Therefore don't despise the chastening of the Almighty. For he wounds, and binds up. He injures, and his hands make whole. He will deliver you in six troubles; yes, in seven no evil will touch you."

— Job 5:17–19 WEB

Devotional Insight

El Shaddai is the God whose correction is not destruction but restoration. The Almighty wounds only to heal more deeply. He allows shaking only to establish us more securely. Through discipline, He shapes character, purifies motives, and strengthens spiritual resilience. Job's friend unknowingly speaks a timeless truth: God Almighty delivers, protects, binds up, and makes whole. For believers today, El Shaddai stands as the One who both forms and defends us. His sufficiency covers us in trouble, and His power rescues us from danger. The Almighty's discipline is evidence of His commitment to our growth, not His rejection. Every wound He allows becomes a gateway to deeper wholeness.

Prayer

El Shaddai, God Almighty, I submit myself to Your loving correction and strengthening power. You are the God who shapes me with wisdom and restores me with compassion. I thank You that every challenging season is held within Your sufficiency and governed by Your goodness.

God Almighty, where You have allowed discomfort, let healing also flow. Where You have exposed weaknesses, let Your power fill the gap. Bind up every wound with Your tender hands. Restore joy where pain has lingered. Restore clarity where confusion once had a voice.

El Shaddai, deliver me from every trouble, both seen and unseen. In the battles I face, stand as my defender. In the trials that surround me, be my shield. Let no evil touch me or my family. Cover my household under Your mighty wings and guard every path we walk.

Lord, strengthen my heart to embrace Your forming process. Teach me to trust Your methods and Your timing. Let every adversity refine me rather than break me. Shape my character until it reflects Your beauty and strength.

El Shaddai, let Your sustaining power carry me through every season. May all discipline become a doorway to deeper maturity and greater intimacy with You. In Jesus' name, Amen.

10

Pierced Yet Preserved by the Almighty

"For the arrows of the Almighty are within me. My spirit drinks up their poison. The terrors of God set themselves in array against me."
— Job 6:4 WEB

Devotional Insight

Job's words are raw and unfiltered, revealing the depth of human anguish. Yet even in his confusion, he acknowledges God as El Shaddai—the Almighty whose presence is inescapable, even in pain. Job misinterprets his suffering, but the truth behind his cry remains: El Shaddai is present in affliction, not absent. The Almighty does not abandon His own; He upholds, protects, and sustains them even when emotions scream otherwise. For believers today, this Name reassures us that God's sufficiency surrounds us in seasons where we cannot understand His ways. He is mighty enough to handle our grief and faithful enough to carry us through it. Pain does not indicate His absence—it becomes the place where His sustaining power is most needed.

Prayer

El Shaddai, God Almighty, I come before You with every burden too heavy for my heart. You see the places where pain feels overwhelming and where discouragement has pressed upon my soul. Thank You that even when I cannot understand, You remain present, strong, and unchanging.

God Almighty, sustain me in every emotional battle. Lift me when despair tries to pull me downward. Let Your sufficiency surround the wounded parts of my heart. Where sharp pains pierce my spirit, let Your healing presence bring comfort. Where fear whispers lies, silence every voice that contradicts Your truth.

El Shaddai, carry me through seasons that feel dark or heavy. Do not let sorrow drown me. Do not let confusion define me. Be my strength when I have none. Be my courage when I feel afraid. Be my anchor when storms shake everything around me.

Lord, preserve my faith in the midst of adversity. Let Your power keep me from collapsing under the weight of discouragement. Uphold me with Your mighty hand. Let me sense Your nearness even when my emotions say otherwise. Surround my family with Your comfort, and let Your peace rest upon every heart.

El Shaddai, rise within me as the God who sustains, the God who heals, and the God who carries His people through every trial. Let my life declare that even in pain, the Almighty is present and faithful. In Jesus' name, Amen.

11

Restored by the Almighty's Justice

"Does God pervert justice? Or does the Almighty pervert righteousness? If your children have sinned against him, he has delivered them into the hand of their disobedience. If you want to seek God diligently, make your supplication to the Almighty. If you were pure and upright, surely now he would awaken for you, and make the habitation of your righteousness prosperous. Though your beginning was small, yet your latter end would greatly increase."
— Job 8:3–7 WEB

Devotional Insight

El Shaddai is revealed here as the God whose justice is perfect and whose restoration is unstoppable. Even though Job's friends misunderstood his situation, the truth remains that the Almighty does not distort justice and He never abandons the righteous. El Shaddai is the God who awakens on behalf of His people, who restores what was diminished, and who increases what seemed too small to matter. His sufficiency ensures that no beginning—no matter how humble—remains insignificant when placed in His hands. For believers today, this Name assures us that God Almighty oversees our story with righteousness, mercy, and power. He restores, He prospers, and He increases according to His perfect justice.

Prayer

El Shaddai, God Almighty, I lift my heart before You in deep gratitude that You are a God of justice who never perverts righteousness. Your ways are pure, Your judgments perfect, and Your compassion unfailing. Today I surrender every unjust situation, every misjudgment, and every loss into Your mighty hands.

God Almighty, awaken for me as You promised. Let Your righteousness go before me and Your justice defend me. Where my beginnings have been small, let Your increase arise. Where the enemy has sought to diminish me, cause Your divine restoration to overflow. Let every area of my life that seems unimpressive or overlooked become a testimony of Your multiplying power.

El Shaddai, prosper the habitation of righteousness within me. Establish purity of heart and clarity of purpose. Strengthen my family under the covering of Your justice. Let no accusation, no confusion, and no misalignment stand against what You have ordained.

Lord, release increase in every area connected to my destiny—spiritual, emotional, relational, financial, and generational. Let my latter end greatly surpass my beginning. Let every step forward be marked by the sufficiency of Your power and the tenderness of Your shepherding love.

El Shaddai, vindicate, restore, and elevate according to Your perfect righteousness. In Jesus' name, Amen.

12

Unsearchable Greatness of the Almighty

"Can you fathom the mystery of God? Or can you probe the limits of the Almighty?"
— Job 11:7 WEB

Devotional Insight

El Shaddai is the God whose greatness is beyond human comprehension. His wisdom has no measure, His power has no boundary, and His purposes stretch further than the mind can imagine. Job's friend speaks a profound truth— the Almighty is infinitely beyond the reach of human analysis, yet lovingly near to His people. For believers today, this Name invites us to trust rather than strive to understand everything. El Shaddai is unsearchable, yet knowable; infinite, yet intimate. When we cannot trace His ways, we anchor ourselves in His character. The unfathomable greatness of God Almighty assures us that no situation is too complex, too dark, or too overwhelming for Him to masterfully redeem.

Prayer

El Shaddai, God Almighty, I bow before Your unsearchable greatness. You are the God whose wisdom cannot be measured, whose power cannot be contained, and whose understanding surpasses the limits of time, space, and human thought. Today I rest in the majesty of who You are.

God Almighty, when my mind reaches its limits, Your power continues. When my understanding falters, Your wisdom prevails. Teach me to trust You in mysteries, to lean into Your sufficiency when the path ahead seems unclear. Let the wonder of Your greatness fill my heart with peace.

El Shaddai, strengthen me to surrender every burden I do not understand. Remind me that even what is hidden from me is still held in Your perfect hands. Replace anxiety with awe. Replace striving with stillness. Replace confusion with confidence in Your unchanging nature.

Lord, let my family experience the nearness of Your limitless presence. Overshadow every difficult situation with Your incomprehensible might. Let Your wisdom guide our decisions, Your power sustain our journey, and Your sovereignty calm every fear.

El Shaddai, I worship You not because I understand everything You do, but because I know who You are—faithful, mighty, tender, and eternally sufficient. In Jesus' name, Amen.

13

Refined by the Almighty

> "If you return to the Almighty, you will be built up, if you put away unrighteousness far from your tents. Lay your treasure in the dust, the gold of Ophir among the stones of the brooks. The Almighty will be your treasure, and precious silver to you."
> — Job 22:23–25 WEB

Devotional Insight

El Shaddai calls His people back to Himself as their true treasure. He is the One who builds, restores, and strengthens the believer from the inside out. While Job's friend speaks with incomplete understanding, the truth stands: when we turn wholeheartedly to the Almighty, we rediscover sufficiency, stability, and value rooted in God rather than earthly wealth. El Shaddai becomes the believer's treasure—the source of strength, the wellspring of hope, and the foundation of lasting security. His sufficiency is greater than any riches, and His presence enriches life far beyond material blessings. To return to El Shaddai is to exchange fragility for divine strength and temporary gain for eternal value.

Prayer

El Shaddai, God Almighty, I return to You with my whole heart. You are my treasure, my source, my everlasting sufficiency. I lay down every false reliance, every earthly idol, and every pursuit that has distracted me from Your presence. Build me up again according to Your perfect design.

God Almighty, cleanse my life from anything that does not reflect Your holiness. Purify my motives, refine my desires, and align my choices with Your will. Let unrighteousness find no place in my home or in my heart. Establish Your righteousness as the foundation upon which my family stands.

El Shaddai, become my wealth—my wisdom, my strength, my supply, my peace. Teach me to value Your presence above every earthly possession. Let my confidence rest not in what I can accumulate, but in the sufficiency of who You are.

Lord, rebuild every part of my life that has been weakened, discouraged, or torn down. Establish me in stability, resilience, and strength. Let Your sufficiency elevate every area where lack once ruled.

El Shaddai, be my precious silver, my enduring treasure, my inexhaustible supply. Let my life shine with the richness of Your presence and the beauty of Your transforming power. In Jesus' name, Amen.

14

Kept in the Knowledge of the Almighty

"I will teach you about the hand of God. I will not conceal what the Almighty does."
— Job 27:11 WEB

Devotional Insight

El Shaddai works in ways that shape, reveal, and establish His power in the lives of His people. Even in Job's suffering, he is confident that the Almighty is active, intentional, and sovereign. To know El Shaddai is to learn His ways—to recognize His hand at work even when the circumstances are difficult. God Almighty is not silent, distant, or inactive; He is present, guiding, sustaining, and teaching. For believers today, the Almighty reveals His hand through His Word, His Spirit, His dealings, and His faithfulness. We are invited to learn His patterns, trust His timing, and rest in His sufficiency.

Prayer

El Shaddai, God Almighty, open my heart to be taught by Your hand. Let me recognize Your movements, Your guidance, and Your sustaining power in every area of my life. You are never absent, never distant, never inactive. I praise You for the ways You lead, protect, and shape me.

God Almighty, teach me to discern Your hand at work. Let me see Your fingerprints in the ordinary and Your majesty in the unexpected. Help me recognize Your mercy, even in discipline; Your goodness, even in delays; and Your strength, even in my weakness.

El Shaddai, guide my family with Your wisdom. Reveal Your hand in our decisions, in our relationships, in our dreams, and in our daily steps. Let nothing You are doing be hidden from us. Give us spiritual perception to understand Your dealings and respond with obedience.

Lord, where I have misunderstood Your movements, grant clarity. Where I have resisted Your shaping, grant surrender. Where I have doubted Your intentions, restore confidence in Your goodness.

El Shaddai, let the testimony of my life declare that the Almighty is active, faithful, and perfectly wise. Teach me continually. Lead me deeply. Keep me securely in the knowledge of Your unchanging hand. In Jesus' name, Amen.

15

Breathed Upon by the Almighty

"The Spirit of God has made me, and the breath of the Almighty gives me life."
— Job 33:4 WEB

Devotional Insight

El Shaddai is the life-giving God whose breath sustains every moment of existence. The Almighty forms, shapes, and animates our lives with His Spirit. His breath is not merely oxygen—it is divine empowerment, spiritual vitality, and sustaining grace. Every renewal, every revival, every strengthening in the believer's life comes from the breath of the Almighty. El Shaddai is the God who revives weary hearts, restores failing strength, and breathes fresh life into dreams, callings, and destinies. His sufficiency is displayed in the ongoing miracle of His breath sustaining us daily.

Prayer

El Shaddai, God Almighty, breathe upon me today. Let the breath that formed me, revived me, and sustained me fill every weary part of my being. You are the God who gives life—not only at birth but in every moment that follows. I welcome the fresh breath of Your Spirit.

God Almighty, revive what has grown tired within me. Strengthen my spirit, renew my mind, and awaken my faith. Let every place burdened by disappointment or fatigue receive Your life-giving breath. Let Your Spirit quicken my inner man with divine vitality.

El Shaddai, breathe upon my family. Let Your life flow into our relationships, our decisions, our health, and our purpose. Where hope has faded, let Your breath restore it. Where discouragement has settled, let Your breath lift it. Where dreams have dimmed, let Your breath ignite them again.

Lord, let the breath of the Almighty empower me to walk in holiness, courage, and obedience. Fill me with fresh passion for Your presence. Let Your life radiate through me to everyone connected to my destiny.

El Shaddai, continually breathe Your sufficiency into my life. Animate every step I take, saturate every assignment I carry, and revive every dream You have planted within me. In Jesus' name, Amen.

16

Shielded by the Almighty

"But you, Yahweh, are a shield around me, my glory, and the one who lifts up my head."
— Psalm 3:3 WEB

Devotional Insight

El Shaddai reveals Himself as the God who surrounds His people with protective strength. He is not a distant defender but a shield that encircles, upholds, and lifts. When David fled from enemies who seemed overwhelming, he discovered the Almighty as the One who covers vulnerability, restores dignity, and lifts the weary soul. For believers today, the Almighty remains our shield—strong enough to block every attack, tender enough to lift our heads when discouragement presses down. El Shaddai is both protection and restoration, the sufficiency that guards our hearts and the glory that reawakens hope.

Prayer

El Shaddai, God Almighty, I thank You for being the shield that surrounds every part of my life. You guard my mind, my heart, my family, and my destiny with unmatched strength. No threat, no accusation, no darkness can penetrate the divine defense of Your presence.

God Almighty, lift my head where it has bowed under the weight of pressure, fear, or discouragement. Restore honor where shame has attempted to settle. Restore strength where weariness has lingered. Let the glory of Your sufficiency shine over my life and illuminate every place that has felt dimmed by adversity.

El Shaddai, shield my family from harm. Protect us from spiritual attacks, emotional wounds, relational fractures, and every assault of the enemy. Surround our home with Your impenetrable might. Let peace reign within our walls and joy flourish under Your covering.

Lord, be my confidence in every battle. Remind me daily that I am not exposed or unprotected; I am encompassed by the Almighty. Where fear tries to whisper lies, let Your truth rise with power. Where anxiety attempts to grip my heart, let Your presence bring calm.

El Shaddai, continue to lift my head and remind me that You are for me, with me, and around me. Let my life declare that the Almighty is my shield and my glory forever. In Jesus' name, Amen.

17

Strengthened by the Almighty

"As for God, his way is perfect. Yahweh's word is tried. He is a shield to all those who take refuge in him. For who is God, except Yahweh? Who is a rock, besides our God? The God who arms me with strength, and makes my way perfect."
— Psalm 18:30–32 WEB

Devotional Insight

El Shaddai, the Almighty One, empowers His people with strength that does not originate in human ability. David recognizes that God Himself becomes the warrior's endurance, stability, and perfection. El Shaddai is the God who arms His people—equipping them with strength, stability, and supernatural resilience. His sufficiency fills the believer with the ability to accomplish what would otherwise be impossible. For believers today, this Name assures us that the path God calls us to walk is one He also empowers us to complete. El Shaddai supplies perfect strength, perfect protection, and perfect guidance.

Prayer

El Shaddai, God Almighty, I honor You as the source of all true strength. You are my Rock, my Refuge, and my Shield. Your ways are flawless, Your Word unshakable, and Your power unmatched. Today I receive the divine strength You freely pour into my life.

God Almighty, arm me with supernatural strength for every assignment, challenge, and season ahead. Strengthen my resolve where I feel tempted to retreat. Empower my spirit where weakness has attempted to settle. Let Your sufficiency fill every place my human capacity ends.

El Shaddai, make my way perfect—not by removing obstacles, but by aligning my steps with Your will. Guide me with clarity. Steady my feet on uneven ground. Protect me from missteps and wrong paths. Let Your wisdom illuminate every decision.

Lord, shield my family under Your mighty wings. Arm each of us with strength for our unique journeys. Let Your power stabilize our emotions, reinforce our faith, and anchor our hope. Surround our home with Your peace and fill our hearts with courage.

El Shaddai, empower me to overcome every limitation. Let Your strength be visible in my accomplishments, my endurance, and my victories. May my life testify that the Almighty is the One who strengthens and perfects His people. In Jesus' name, Amen.

18

Victory Under the Almighty's Voice

"Yahweh sat enthroned at the Flood. Yes, Yahweh sits as King forever. Yahweh will give strength to his people. Yahweh will bless his people with peace."

— Psalm 29:10–11 WEB

Devotional Insight

El Shaddai reigns as the eternal King whose authority governs every storm and season. Even in the chaos of the Flood, God remained enthroned—unshaken, sovereign, and ruling with absolute might. The Almighty gives strength and peace to His people because He Himself is unmovable. His sufficiency is not affected by circumstances. For believers today, the Almighty's rule means that no storm has the power to dethrone God or derail His promises. El Shaddai imparts strength for the battle and peace for the aftermath. He reigns forever and sustains His people with eternal stability.

Prayer

El Shaddai, God Almighty, I worship You as the eternal King who sits enthroned above every storm, every crisis, and every shifting circumstance. Your reign is unchanging, Your authority unchallenged, and Your sufficiency unlimited.

God Almighty, give me strength as You promised. Strength to stand when winds blow fiercely. Strength to trust when uncertainty rises. Strength to persevere when challenges intensify. Let Your endless might fill me with unshakable resilience.

El Shaddai, bless me with Your peace—the peace that calms storms, settles anxious thoughts, and silences every tormenting fear. Let Your peace rest upon my home, saturating every room with divine tranquility. Let it guard our hearts and minds with supernatural stillness.

Lord, because You are enthroned forever, my life is secure. Let this truth anchor my soul when circumstances shift. Let Your sovereignty steady my emotions and renew my faith. Reign over every decision, every transition, and every challenge in my life.

El Shaddai, reign in my family. Establish Your peace in our relationships and Your strength in our spirits. Let Your presence be our confidence and Your authority our assurance.

I declare that my life belongs to the God who sits as King forever—El Shaddai, my strength and my peace. In Jesus' name, Amen.

# 19

Daily Sustained by the Almighty

"Blessed be the Lord, who daily bears our burdens, even the God who is our salvation. God is to us a God of deliverance. To Yahweh, the Lord, belongs escape from death."
— Psalm 68:19–20 WEB

Devotional Insight

El Shaddai carries His people daily. He does not offer an occasional lifting but a continual sustaining. The Almighty bears burdens, delivers from danger, and rescues from threats that could destroy us. His sufficiency is not seasonal—it is constant, consistent, and unchanging. For believers, this means we never walk a single day unsupported. El Shaddai shoulders what we cannot carry and saves us in ways we do not always see. His deliverance is comprehensive and His salvation ongoing. He is the God who bears, carries, rescues, and sustains.

Prayer

El Shaddai, God Almighty, I bless Your Name for carrying me every single day. When I am aware of it and when I am not, You lift burdens from my shoulders and sustain me with Your strength. You are the God of my salvation, my daily help, and my unfailing deliverer.

God Almighty, I release every weight I have been holding—emotional burdens, mental pressures, spiritual battles, and physical strains. Carry them as only You can. Lift them from me and replace them with Your peace. Where I feel overwhelmed, let Your sufficiency rise and steady my soul.

El Shaddai, deliver me from every assignment of darkness. Break the chains of fear, anxiety, and discouragement. Rescue my family from every threat—seen or unseen. Let Your mighty hand surround us with protection and Your deliverance secure every area of our lives.

Lord, be my escape from death—not just physical death, but every form of decay, destruction, and despair that the enemy attempts to plant. Let life, hope, and renewal flow from Your presence.

El Shaddai, thank You for carrying me today, tomorrow, and every day to come. Let my life be a continual testimony that the Almighty bears His people tenderly and powerfully. In Jesus' name, Amen.

20

Dwelling Under the Almighty's Shadow

"He who dwells in the secret place of the Most High will rest in the shadow of the Almighty."
— Psalm 91:1 WEB

Devotional Insight

El Shaddai is the God whose presence becomes a refuge, a hiding place, and a covering of supernatural protection. To dwell under His shadow is to live within the radius of His sufficiency. The Almighty's nearness becomes rest, His presence becomes shelter, and His strength becomes security. For believers today, this Name assures us that intimacy with God produces protection that cannot be gained any other way. El Shaddai covers, shields, guards, and sustains those who draw near. His shadow is not dark but safe—a place where fear dissipates and peace reigns.

Prayer

El Shaddai, God Almighty, I enter the secret place of Your presence and rest under the shadow of Your wings. You are my refuge, my shelter, and my eternal covering. In You I find rest that the world cannot give and peace that circumstances cannot steal.

God Almighty, draw me deeper into the place of abiding. Let my heart remain anchored in Your presence. Let my thoughts be filled with Your truth and my spirit saturated with Your peace. Remove every distraction that tries to pull me away from the safety of Your shadow.

El Shaddai, cover my family with Your protective presence. Let Your shadow rest upon our home, shielding us from danger, disease, disaster, and every scheme of the enemy. Fortify our minds with peace and guard our hearts with Your strength.

Lord, teach me to dwell—not visit—in the secret place. Let Your presence become my habitation, my resting place, my constant refuge. Let fear melt away as I remain under the shelter of the Almighty.

El Shaddai, overshadow every part of my life with Your sufficiency. Let Your protective covering surround my steps, my decisions, my relationships, and my destiny. I belong to the One whose shadow is life, peace, and unshakable security. In Jesus' name, Amen.

21

Renewed by Almighty Strength

"He gives power to the weak. He increases the strength of him who has no might. Even the youths faint and get weary, and the young men utterly fall; but those who wait for Yahweh will renew their strength. They will mount up with wings like eagles; they will run, and not be weary; they will walk, and not faint."

— Isaiah 40:29–31 WEB

Devotional Insight

El Shaddai reveals Himself as the inexhaustible source of strength for those who wait upon Him. Human vigor fades, natural energy declines, and willpower eventually collapses—but the Almighty infuses supernatural endurance into those who draw near to Him. He renews strength, elevates perspective, and empowers movement. The weak are not dismissed; they are revived. Those without might are not forgotten; they are strengthened. El Shaddai meets the believer in exhaustion and transforms it into soaring resilience. His sufficiency ensures that every step, run, and rise is empowered by His everlasting strength.

Prayer

El Shaddai, God Almighty, I bow before You in grateful surrender, confessing my need for Your strength. You are the One who renews, restores, and revives. I thank You that Your power is made perfect in my weakness and that You never grow weary in giving strength to Your children.

God Almighty, breathe fresh endurance into my spirit. Lift me from the weight of fatigue and refresh my inner man with divine power. Renew my strength so I may rise above every challenge with eagle-like vision and grace. Empower my steps so I may run without weariness and walk without fainting.

El Shaddai, strengthen my family with Your everlasting might. Where they feel exhausted, restore them. Where hope has dimmed, rekindle it. Where burdens have drained their energy, infuse them with Your sustaining power.

Lord, lift my perspective. Let me see my circumstances from heavenly heights rather than earthly limitations. Teach me to wait upon You—not passively, but in expectant surrender that draws strength from Your presence.

El Shaddai, let every day of my life be lived in the overflow of Your sufficiency. Strengthen me to accomplish what You have ordained, to endure what You have allowed, and to rise into what You have promised. In Jesus' name, Amen.

22

Nourished by the Almighty

> "You will also drink the milk of the nations, and will nurse from royal breasts. Then you will know that I, Yahweh, am your Savior, your Redeemer, the Mighty One of Jacob."
> — Isaiah 60:16 WEB

Devotional Insight

El Shaddai is the Mighty One of Jacob, the God who nourishes, sustains, and provides abundance from unexpected sources. In this prophetic promise, God reveals that He Himself is the sustainer of His people, supplying provision that flows from His covenant favor. To "nurse" from royal abundance is to partake of provision that only the Almighty can orchestrate. Believers today experience El Shaddai as the One who feeds their souls, strengthens their hearts, and provides from heavenly resources. His sufficiency is seen not only in strength but also in tender nourishment.

Prayer

El Shaddai, God Almighty, I praise You as the Mighty One of Jacob, the God who nourishes and sustains His people with abundant provision. You are the source of everything I need—spiritually, emotionally, physically, and relationally.

God Almighty, feed me with what comes from You alone. Let my soul drink deeply of Your presence, Your wisdom, and Your truth. Nourish every dry place within me. Restore vitality where depletion has taken hold. Let Your divine provision flow into my family like refreshing milk that strengthens and satisfies.

El Shaddai, open doors of favor and provision that only Your hand can orchestrate. Let resources come from unexpected places, and let royal provision be made manifest in my life. Supply every need according to Your riches in glory. Let my dependence rest fully on You—not on people, systems, or circumstances.

Lord, redeem every area where lack or insufficiency has lingered. Establish the testimony of Your saving and redeeming power in my household. Let us know You as Savior, Redeemer, and Mighty Provider.

El Shaddai, let abundance flow—not merely for survival, but for flourishing. Make my life a living witness that God Almighty nourishes His people with excellence and tenderness. In Jesus' name, Amen.

23

Awed by the Almighty's Voice

> "When they went, I heard the noise of their wings like the noise of great waters, and like the voice of the Almighty, a noise of tumult like the noise of an army. When they stood, they let down their wings."
> — Ezekiel 1:24 WEB

Devotional Insight

The voice of El Shaddai is described as thunderous, majestic, and commanding—like the roar of many waters and the movement of an army. His voice carries authority, power, and unmistakable presence. When the Almighty speaks, creation responds, angels stand still, and the atmosphere shifts. For believers today, El Shaddai's voice brings direction, correction, encouragement, and revelation. His Word awakens the spirit, strengthens faith, and silences fear. The same Almighty whose voice Ezekiel encountered still speaks with unmatched authority into the lives of His people.

Prayer

El Shaddai, God Almighty, let Your voice thunder over my life with clarity and power. I long to hear Your direction, to sense Your presence, and to respond to Your call with awe and obedience. Your voice is life, strength, and authority to my soul.

God Almighty, speak into the noise around me. Silence every voice of fear, confusion, and distraction. Let Your voice rise above every competing sound. As the roar of many waters commands attention, let Your Word command my path and settle my heart.

El Shaddai, align my family under the power of Your voice. Speak peace where anxiety has tried to grip us. Speak order where chaos has attempted to reign. Speak hope where discouragement has lingered. Let Your voice determine our decisions and guide our steps.

Lord, open my ears to hear You clearly. Let every part of my being become sensitive to Your whispers and responsive to Your commands. Let the authority of Your voice break every chain and dispel every lie formed against me.

El Shaddai, speak with power, speak with love, and speak with purpose. Let my life resonate with the sound of the Almighty and reflect the glory of Your presence. In Jesus' name, Amen.

24

Stirred by the Almighty's Movement

> "A voice came from above the expanse that was over their heads; when they stood, they let down their wings. The sound of the wings of the cherubim was heard even to the outer court, as the voice of God Almighty when he speaks."
> — Ezekiel 10:5 WEB

Devotional Insight

El Shaddai moves with audible majesty, and His activity reverberates through the atmosphere. His voice carries authority and unmistakable presence, stirring heaven and earth. When the Almighty speaks, nothing remains unaffected—angels respond, creation aligns, and His people experience His weighty glory. For believers today, El Shaddai still moves with power, and His voice still shapes destinies. His presence interrupts complacency, awakens purpose, and draws us into deeper reverence. The Almighty's voice is a reminder that He is ever-active, ever-present, and ever-engaged with His creation.

Prayer

El Shaddai, God Almighty, let the sound of Your voice echo through my life with holy power. Stir my spirit with Your presence. Let Your movement awaken every dormant area within me. Speak with authority that breaks through stagnation and awakens divine purpose.

God Almighty, let Your presence fill my home like the sound of angelic wings—powerful, unmistakable, and holy. Move through every room, bringing peace, purity, and the weight of Your glory. Let every opposing force be silenced in the presence of the Almighty.

El Shaddai, teach my heart to stand in reverence before You. Let my spirit recognize the moments when You move, speak, or shift the atmosphere. Make me sensitive to Your promptings and obedient to Your commands.

Lord, let Your voice override every voice of discouragement, deception, or distraction. Let Your Word shape my decisions, direct my steps, and guard my thoughts. When You speak, let everything in me bow in surrender.

El Shaddai, move mightily in my life and family. Let Your voice awaken us, align us, and anoint us. Let us become vessels through whom Your glory is revealed. In Jesus' name, Amen.

25

Roaring Deliverance of the Almighty

"Yahweh will roar from Zion, and thunder from Jerusalem; and the heavens and the earth will shake; but Yahweh will be a refuge to his people, and a stronghold to the children of Israel."
— Joel 3:16 WEB

Devotional Insight

El Shaddai is revealed as the mighty defender who roars on behalf of His people. His roar shakes heaven and earth, disrupting the plans of the enemy and establishing divine justice. Yet to His people, this same roar becomes refuge and strength. The Almighty is both terrifying to darkness and comforting to His children. For believers today, this means God is actively fighting for us. His power dismantles opposition, His voice overturns injustice, and His presence becomes a fortress of safety. El Shaddai is the God who thunders against our enemies but shelters us in His love.

Prayer

El Shaddai, God Almighty, roar over my life with Your delivering power. Shake the heavens and the earth on my behalf. Let every opposing force tremble at the sound of Your voice. You are my refuge, my stronghold, my everlasting protection.

God Almighty, thunder against every attack formed against me and my family. Shatter every plan of darkness. Scatter every enemy rising in secret. Let the roar of Your authority dismantle every scheme designed to bring destruction or delay.

El Shaddai, be my refuge. Surround me with the impenetrable walls of Your presence. Let Your peace fill my heart and guard my mind. Let Your strength sustain me through every battle and Your wisdom guide me through every decision.

Lord, fight for my family. Defend us from spiritual attacks, emotional pressures, and relational disturbances. Let Your roar silence the voice of fear, discouragement, and confusion. Establish us in the safety of Your covenant love.

El Shaddai, let the sound of Your deliverance echo through every part of my life. Roar until chains break, paths open, and victory manifests. You are the Almighty who defends, protects, and preserves Your people. In Jesus' name, Amen.

26

All Things Possible with the Almighty

> "Looking at them, Jesus said, 'With men this is impossible, but with God all things are possible.'"
> — Matthew 19:26 WEB

Devotional Insight

El Shaddai—God Almighty—is the God of the impossible. Jesus reveals that what human strength, wisdom, resources, and effort cannot accomplish becomes attainable under the sufficiency of the Almighty. El Shaddai operates beyond limitation, beyond natural law, beyond human expectation. His power makes a way where none exists, resolves what cannot be solved, heals what seems incurable, and restores what appears beyond repair. For the believer, this Name ignites hope, faith, and holy expectation. El Shaddai is the God who turns impossibilities into testimonies of His might, proving He alone is sufficient.

Prayer

El Shaddai, God Almighty, I praise You as the One who makes impossibilities bow. Nothing is too hard for You, too broken for You to restore, or too far gone for You to redeem. I bring before You every situation that seems impossible, knowing that Your power transforms impossibility into divine fulfillment.

God Almighty, let Your sufficiency overshadow every limitation in my life. Where resources have failed, supply abundantly. Where strength has run out, renew supernaturally. Where solutions are absent, create new pathways by Your power. I choose to believe Your Word above every natural circumstance.

El Shaddai, breathe possibility into my dreams, my assignments, my family, and my destiny. Restore what is broken. Heal what is wounded. Revive what has grown cold. Let Your power challenge every lie that whispers "It cannot change."

Lord, let impossible breakthroughs arise in my family. Salvations, healings, reconciliations, financial turnaround, emotional restoration—do what only the Almighty can do. Let our testimony shine with the unmistakable imprint of Your power.

El Shaddai, strengthen my faith. Teach me to expect the miraculous, to stand on Your Word without wavering, and to trust You even when I cannot see the outcome. You are the God for whom nothing is impossible, and I rest in Your mighty sufficiency. In Jesus' name, Amen.

27

Power Perfected Through the Almighty

> "He has said to me, 'My grace is sufficient for you, for my power is made perfect in weakness.' Most gladly therefore I will rather glory in my weaknesses, that the power of Christ may rest on me. Therefore I take pleasure in weaknesses, insults, necessities, persecutions, and distresses for Christ's sake; for when I am weak, then am I strong."
> — 2 Corinthians 12:9–10 WEB

Devotional Insight

El Shaddai displays His might not by removing weakness but by filling it with His power. His grace is not merely adequate—it is all-sufficient, overflowing, and perfecting. In weakness, the believer discovers the tender strength of the Almighty, who rests upon those who acknowledge their need. God Almighty transforms frailty into strength, insufficiency into testimony, and struggle into glory. The believer's weakness becomes the platform upon which El Shaddai displays His unmatched sufficiency.

Prayer

El Shaddai, God Almighty, I come before You embracing my weakness, for it is the place where Your power rests most beautifully. Thank You that Your grace is more than enough—that it not only covers me but empowers me, strengthens me, and perfects me.

God Almighty, let Your power fill every weak place in my life. Where I feel insufficient, be my sufficiency. Where I feel fragile, be my strength. Where I struggle to endure, be the endurance that carries me. Rest upon me with the fullness of Your might.

El Shaddai, empower me to face every difficulty with confidence in Your grace. Transform insults, needs, pressures, and trials into opportunities for Your glory to be revealed. Let my weakness become the doorway for Your strength to shine through.

Lord, let Your power overshadow my family. Fill every area where we feel overwhelmed. Strengthen our spirits, renew our minds, and fortify our hearts. Let Your grace be the covering over our home and the strength within our walls.

El Shaddai, let the world see through my life that the Almighty shows His greatness in human weakness. Let every step I take be marked not by my ability but by Your power resting upon me. In Jesus' name, Amen.

28

Abundantly Supplied by the Almighty

> "Now to him who is able to do exceedingly abundantly above all that we ask or think, according to the power that works in us, to him be the glory in the assembly and in Christ Jesus to all generations forever and ever. Amen."
> — Ephesians 3:20–21 WEB

Devotional Insight

El Shaddai exceeds every human measurement. His sufficiency is beyond imagination, beyond requests, and beyond comprehension. The Almighty works not only around us but within us—His power operating in believers to accomplish supernatural outcomes. El Shaddai does exceedingly, abundantly, and immeasurably more than what faith dares to articulate. For believers today, this Name inspires bold prayers, confident expectation, and unwavering trust in God's limitless ability. His power is not restricted—it overflows.

Prayer

El Shaddai, God Almighty, I honor You as the God who does exceedingly and abundantly beyond anything I can ask, think, or imagine. Your ability is limitless, Your power unmatched, and Your generosity overwhelming. I surrender every small expectation and embrace the vastness of Your sufficiency.

God Almighty, let Your power work mightily within me. Expand my capacity to believe, receive, and obey. Stretch my faith beyond the boundaries of fear, past disappointment, and above natural reasoning. Let the abundance of Your power flow unhindered through my life.

El Shaddai, release overflow into my family. Let blessings exceed expectation, let breakthroughs surpass prayer requests, and let miracles unfold in ways only the Almighty can orchestrate. Do above what I have asked concerning our health, finances, relationships, and destiny.

Lord, reveal the greatness of Your power within me. Let Christ be glorified through my life. Let Your glory shine in my household and extend to future generations.

El Shaddai, do abundantly. Do exceedingly. Do immeasurably. Let every work of Your power bring honor to Your Name and testify that the Almighty still works wonders. In Jesus' name, Amen.

29

Saved Completely by the Almighty

"Therefore he is also able to save to the uttermost those who draw near to God through him, seeing he lives forever to make intercession for them."
— Hebrews 7:25 WEB

Devotional Insight

El Shaddai is the God who saves fully, completely, and eternally. Through Christ, the Almighty extends a salvation that reaches the deepest places of need and continues without end. Jesus intercedes forever, ensuring that the believer is upheld, preserved, and perfected. Salvation is not fragile; it is fortified by the eternal life and intercession of the Son of God. For believers, this Name gives assurance, confidence, and unwavering peace. El Shaddai does not do partial work—He saves to the uttermost.

Prayer

El Shaddai, God Almighty, I rejoice that You save completely and eternally. Through Christ's intercession, my soul is secure, my destiny is protected, and my salvation is continually upheld by divine power. You are the God who finishes what You begin.

God Almighty, let the saving power of Christ penetrate every area of my life. Save me from sin's residue, from lingering fears, from hidden wounds, and from every attack of darkness. Save my family to the uttermost—spiritually, emotionally, mentally, and physically.

El Shaddai, let Christ's eternal intercession prevail over every accusation of the enemy. Silence every voice of condemnation. Overturn every word spoken against my destiny. Let the blood of Jesus speak louder than every failing or weakness.

Lord, draw me nearer to You daily. Let the intimacy of fellowship deepen. Let Your Spirit continually transform me into the likeness of Christ. Let my life reflect the completeness of Your saving work.

El Shaddai, I rest in the assurance that the Almighty does not abandon, weaken, or falter. You save forever, completely, and with unstoppable power. In Jesus' name, Amen.

30

The Eternal Almighty

"'I am the Alpha and the Omega,' says the Lord God, 'who is and who was and who is to come, the Almighty.'"
— Revelation 1:8 WEB

Devotional Insight

El Shaddai stands outside of time—eternal, unchanging, sovereign. He is the Alpha and the Omega, the beginning and the end, the God who encompasses all existence. His sufficiency spans past, present, and future. Nothing precedes Him, nothing supersedes Him, and nothing escapes His authority. For believers today, this Name anchors us in absolute security. The Almighty governs yesterday's wounds, today's battles, and tomorrow's unknowns with perfect power. His presence is constant, His reign eternal, and His sufficiency complete.

Prayer

El Shaddai, God Almighty, I worship You as the Alpha and the Omega—the God who is, who was, and who is to come. You hold all of time in Your hands and yet You dwell intimately with Your children. I rest in Your eternal sufficiency.

God Almighty, govern every part of my life with Your timeless authority. Heal the wounds of my past, strengthen me in my present, and go ahead of me into my future. Let every day be shaped by the assurance that the Almighty walks with me.

El Shaddai, reign over my family. Cover our beginnings, our transitions, and our endings. Be the author and the finisher of our stories. Let Your eternal nature drive out fear, anxiety, and uncertainty.

Lord, let the revelation of Your Almighty nature anchor my faith. Remind me that nothing arrives before You and nothing escapes beyond You. You are the God who always is—present, powerful, and faithful.

El Shaddai, let my life declare that I belong to the Eternal One, the God whose strength never fades and whose sovereignty never ends. In Jesus' name, Amen.

The Supreme God

◆

אֵל עוֹלָם

EL OLAM

The Everlasting God

Prayers to Anchor Your Life in The Eternal God

CYRIL OPOKU

Preface to Book 6

"Those who know your name will put their trust in you, for you, Yahweh, have not forsaken those who seek you."
— Psalms 9:10 (WEB)

Trust deepens when revelation widens, and Psalm 9:10 declares this timeless truth with quiet authority: those who truly know God's Name learn to rest their confidence in Him. This promise anchors *Book 6—EL OLAM: The Everlasting God.* To know God as **El Olam** is to encounter the One whose faithfulness is not bound by time, whose purposes do not expire, and whose presence does not fade with changing seasons. He is the God who was before beginnings, who stands beyond endings, and who remains constant through every transition of human life.

The Name El Olam reveals a God whose trustworthiness is rooted in eternity. Human assurances often falter because they are tied to circumstance, emotion, or limited vision. But El Olam's reliability flows from His timeless nature. He does not grow weary. He does not revise His character. He does not abandon what He has started. Those who seek Him are never forsaken because He exists beyond the pressures of time that unsettle the human heart. His promises are not rushed, delayed, or endangered—they are eternally secure.

This book invites you to anchor your trust not in immediate outcomes, but in the everlasting faithfulness of God. When life feels uncertain, when answers seem slow, or when seasons stretch longer than expected, El Olam calls you to rest in the assurance that He sees the full horizon. He governs history, generations, and personal journeys with perfect wisdom. As you enter these prayers, allow your soul to settle into the unchanging nature of God. May Psalm 9:10 become more than a verse you read—may it become a truth you live by: the Everlasting God has not forsaken you, and He never will.

To the Praise of His Name!
Cyril O.
(Illinois | December 2025)

Introduction to Book 6

Every believer eventually faces moments when time feels heavy—when waiting stretches faith and tomorrow feels uncertain.

EL OLAM—*The Everlasting God* invites you into a place of steady confidence when life feels rushed, delayed, or unpredictable. El Olam is the God who stands outside of time yet steps fully into your story. He is not pressured by deadlines, threatened by delays, or shaken by seasons of transition. When you know Him as the Everlasting God, you learn to trust not just in what He does, but in who He eternally is.

This volume continues **Part 1 (Books 1–8)** of *The Supreme God* series, building upon the revelations of Elohim, Yahweh, Adonai, El Elyon, and El Shaddai. You are encouraged to journey through the remaining books in Part 1—El Roi and El Gibbor—and then continue into **Part 2 (Books 9–16)**, where the revelation of God expands into His glory, truth, knowledge, holiness, life, heavenly authority, and kingship. Each book reveals another facet of the God whose nature is perfect and whose presence is unending.

As you begin this book, may you encounter El Olam as your anchor—steady, faithful, and eternally trustworthy in every season of your life.

31

Enduring Strength Revealed

"Abraham planted a tamarisk tree in Beersheba, and called there on the name of Yahweh, the Everlasting God."
— Genesis 21:33 WEB

Devotional Insight

El Olam, the Everlasting God, anchors us in a reality far deeper than our fleeting moments and shifting seasons. Abraham called upon Him at a place that marked covenant promise, stability, and divine faithfulness. When believers today encounter uncertainty or transition, El Olam becomes the unchanging One who outlasts every storm and outlives every generation. His purposes remain firm even when our circumstances feel fragile. This Name assures us that nothing about God deteriorates, weakens, or fades with time—His strength, His covenant love, His watchful care, and His sovereign plan remain eternally steady. As you worship Him, you step into the security of a God who is the same before your birth, throughout your journey, and long after your earthly life concludes. His everlasting nature surrounds you, steadies you, and enfolds every detail of your destiny.

Prayer

Everlasting God, El Olam, I come before You with awe, for You remain unchanged while everything around me shifts and moves. You are the God who was, who is, and who forever will be, and I anchor my soul in the certainty of Your eternal presence. Just as Abraham called upon You at Beersheba, I call upon You now in the place of my own need, acknowledging that no season can bind You and no circumstance can limit Your power.

El Olam, steady my heart where life feels fragile. Let Your eternal strength swallow every fear that rises against me. Where transitions unsettle me, let Your everlasting arms uphold me. Where the unknown seems overwhelming, let Your timeless wisdom guide me into peace. You who stand outside of time, step into my time-bound moments and reveal Your unshakeable stability.

I declare that Your covenant concerning me and my family cannot be broken. Your purposes stretch from generation to generation, and Your faithfulness does not weaken with age. Surround my household with Your enduring presence. Let every plan You have spoken over us stand firm, untouched by delay, unaffected by opposition, upheld by Your eternal strength.

Everlasting God, breathe stability into every fluctuating place in my life. Speak peace where anxiety tries to reign.

Let Your eternal nature break every temporal limitation. You are the God whose Word does not expire, whose promises do not shift, and whose goodness does not run dry.

I rest in You, El Olam. Let Your eternal glory saturate my days, align my steps, fortify my mind, and secure my destiny. You are my Everlasting God, and in You, I am safe forever. In Jesus' name, Amen.

32

Everlasting Refuge

"The eternal God is your dwelling place. Underneath are the everlasting arms. He thrust out the enemy from before you, and said, 'Destroy!'"
— Deuteronomy 33:27 WEB

Devotional Insight

El Olam reveals God as both eternal and actively present. His everlasting arms are not symbolic—they are strong, sustaining, defending, and encompassing. The believer experiences Him as a refuge that cannot crumble and a fortress that never weakens. He is the God who lifts, supports, and shields His people, generation after generation. As the Everlasting God, He is not merely ancient; He is eternally powerful and eternally present. This Scripture reveals His protective nature—He goes before you, pushing back what opposes you, empowering you to walk in victory. When you depend on El Olam, you settle into a divine stability that does not shift with circumstances. His eternal arms hold you securely, His eternal purposes guide you, and His eternal authority clears your path.

Prayer

El Olam, Eternal God, I run into the safety of Your everlasting arms today. You are my dwelling place, the refuge that never fades, the stronghold that no enemy can penetrate. I rest in the beauty of Your unending strength. You were God before my story began, and You will remain God long after every chapter of my earthly life has closed. In Your presence, I find the stability my soul desperately needs.

Lord, let Your everlasting arms lift every weight that has been too heavy for me to carry. Hold me where my strength has failed. Steady me where my footing has slipped. Surround me with the assurance that I am upheld by a God who never weakens, never tires, never changes. As You hold me, thrust out every force that rises against Your purposes in my life. Clear my path from opposition—seen or unseen—and release Your command of victory over my battles.

El Olam, I declare that my family dwells in the fortress of Your eternal presence. No enemy can overtake what You surround. No weapon can penetrate what You uphold. Let the might of Your everlasting arms break generational fears, dismantle hidden attacks, and repel every scheme of darkness. You stretch out before us and make our path secure.

Let Your eternal strength manifest in my decisions, my responsibilities, my assignments, and my relationships. Where I have been anxious, be my calm. Where I have been weary, be my renewal. Where I have been uncertain, be my guiding wisdom. I trust Your eternal nature to govern every temporary challenge.

You are my everlasting refuge, my eternal fortress, my unshakeable God. In Jesus' name, Amen.

33

Unchanging Glory

"Also the Strength of Israel will not lie nor repent; for he is not a man, that he should repent."
— 1 Samuel 15:29 WEB

Devotional Insight

El Olam's eternal nature means His character does not mutate, His decisions do not shift with emotion, and His promises never lose validity. This Scripture reveals a God whose integrity is absolute—He does not lie, change His mind, or withdraw what He has established. For believers, this brings profound stability. While human reliability may falter, the everlasting nature of God guarantees unwavering faithfulness. He stands as the Strength of Israel—the One whose Word remains true across centuries, whose decrees outlive every opposition, and whose covenant holds firm. El Olam invites you to trust that what He has spoken concerning your life is anchored in eternity, not circumstance.

Prayer

El Olam, Everlasting God, I honor You as the Strength of my life and the unchanging Anchor of my destiny. You are not like man—Your truth does not waver, Your promises do not dissolve, and Your intentions toward me cannot be overturned. You are steady, reliable, and eternally faithful. I lay every concern at Your feet, trusting not in my feelings but in Your immutable character.

Lord, where I have questioned Your timing, remind me that Your eternal purposes cannot be rushed or delayed. Where I have doubted the fulfillment of Your promises, renew my confidence that Your Word is anchored beyond time and cannot fail. You are the Strength of Israel, and You are the strength of my home, my future, my calling, and my generations.

Let every lie of the enemy collapse under the weight of Your unchanging truth. Let every whisper of doubt be silenced by the certainty of Your everlasting faithfulness. You remain the same in my valleys and on my mountaintops. You remain true when circumstances contradict Your promise. You remain faithful when I falter. Your constancy is my peace.

El Olam, strengthen my family with the assurance that Your covenant stands firm over us. Let Your unchanging nature govern every decision we make. Let Your eternal stability permeate our emotions, finances, relationships, and dreams. Break the power of instability, confusion, and fear. Establish us in the permanence of Your truth.

I surrender again to Your eternal wisdom, trusting that the God who cannot lie is guiding, guarding, and completing every good work in my life. In Jesus' name, Amen.

34

Eternal Goodness Endures

> "Give thanks to Yahweh, for he is good, for his loving kindness endures forever."
> — 1 Chronicles 16:34 WEB

Devotional Insight

El Olam's eternal nature is beautifully revealed in His enduring lovingkindness. His goodness is not seasonal, not fragile, not dependent on human merit—it is forever. This Scripture points the believer to a God whose covenant love continues through every generation. His everlasting kindness meets you in every circumstance, and His goodness remains even in the seasons you don't understand. Because He is eternal, His mercy cannot end and His kindness cannot expire. As the Everlasting God, His goodness toward you is rooted in who He is, not what you've done. Gratitude rises when you realize that the kindness sustaining you today is the same kindness that has carried His people throughout all ages.

Prayer

El Olam, Everlasting God, I lift my voice in gratitude for Your eternal goodness. Your lovingkindness does not flicker like human affection—it burns with the steady intensity of Your everlasting nature. You are good, and Your goodness is not a momentary gift but an unending reality. Today I step into the river of Your mercy that has flowed from generation to generation, washing over me with strength and tenderness.

Lord, saturate my heart with an awareness of Your kindness. Remind me that Your love toward me is not dependent on my perfection but anchored in Your eternal character. Where I have misunderstood You, correct my vision. Where I have felt abandoned, reveal Your unbroken nearness. Where gratitude has drained from my heart, refill me with praise for the God whose mercy never ends.

Let Your everlasting goodness transform my home. Let it soften hardened places, heal broken places, and restore weary places. Let the testimony of Your mercy be evident in my family's story. Let Your goodness follow my children and their children, marking our lineage with covenant kindness.

El Olam, let Your eternal nature overshadow every temporal disappointment, every temporary battle, and every momentary sorrow. Your lovingkindness endures forever—let this truth uproot fear, silence anxiety, and ignite hope. Let my life become a living offering of thanksgiving, grounded in the revelation that You are the same yesterday, today, and forever.

I praise You, Everlasting God, with a heart anchored in Your eternal goodness. In Jesus' name, Amen.

35

Timeless Majesty

"Behold, God is great, and we don't know him.
The number of his years is unsearchable."
— Job 36:26 WEB

Devotional Insight

El Olam, the Everlasting God, dwells beyond the boundaries of human comprehension. His greatness is immeasurable, His wisdom infinite, and His existence eternal. This Scripture reminds the believer that God cannot be confined to human timelines or limited understanding. His eternal nature means He sees the end from the beginning, and He governs life from a perspective untouched by time. When we encounter this Name of God, we are invited into humility and wonder—recognizing that the One who holds our future exists beyond the constraints that trouble us. El Olam assures us that we are led by a God whose majesty spans eternity and whose purposes cannot be hindered.

Prayer

El Olam, Everlasting God, I bow before Your timeless majesty. Your greatness stretches beyond the limits of my understanding. Your years cannot be counted, Your wisdom cannot be measured, and Your power cannot be compared. You exist outside of time, yet You faithfully enter my days, my moments, and my needs with compassion and purpose.

Lord, humble my heart in the presence of Your eternal greatness. Let every anxious thought dissolve as I remember that the God who orchestrates galaxies also orders my steps. You are not surprised by what surprises me. You are not overwhelmed by what overwhelms me. Your eternal perspective governs every detail of my life with flawless precision.

El Olam, let Your majesty settle over my home. Lift our eyes above temporary struggles and let us see life through the lens of Your eternal wisdom. When timelines frustrate us, remind us that You are not bound by them. When impatience tries to overtake us, ground us in trust. When uncertainty threatens our peace, let Your eternal nature become our assurance.

I ask that Your timeless purposes be fulfilled in my family. Align our desires with what You have seen from eternity. Lead us into paths prepared long before our birth. Reveal Yourself to us in deeper ways, drawing us into awe and surrender. Let Your eternal glory illuminate our journey.

You are the Everlasting God, unsearchable in Your years and unfathomable in Your greatness. I rest in Your eternal wisdom and yield to Your perfect timing. In Jesus' name, Amen.

36

King Forever

> "Yahweh is King forever and ever! The nations will perish out of his land."
> — Psalm 10:16 WEB

Devotional Insight

El Olam reveals God as the eternal King whose rule is unending, whose throne is unshakable, and whose dominion outlasts every earthly power. Psalm 10:16 proclaims that while nations rise and fall, God's kingdom has no expiration. For the believer, this eternal Kingship means that God's authority governs every season of life. When instability shakes the world, the Everlasting God remains sovereign and firmly enthroned. His rulership is not threatened by darkness or diminished by time. His reign extends into your family, your calling, and your generations, bringing protection, order, and victory. To trust El Olam is to rest in the certainty that nothing can dethrone the God who reigns forever.

Prayer

El Olam, Everlasting King, I honor You as the One whose throne endures beyond time. You are King forever and ever, ruling with righteousness, power, and unmatched authority. No earthly force can rival Your dominion. No rising darkness can unseat Your sovereignty. You govern the universe with wisdom that spans eternity, and I willingly bow beneath Your unending rule.

Lord, let Your eternal Kingship reign over every corner of my life. Where fear has tried to take territory, let Your kingdom displace it. Where confusion has spoken loudly, silence it with Your royal decrees. Establish the reign of Your peace, Your truth, and Your order in my heart, my home, and my generations. As nations shake around me, let my soul remain anchored in the stability of Your everlasting throne.

El Olam, drive out every spiritual opposition that seeks to occupy ground in my life. Let every force contrary to Your purposes perish from the territory You have assigned me. Push back the shadows that attempt to linger. Let Your kingdom come with authority, cleansing, healing, and establishment.

Over my family, I declare Your everlasting reign. Rule over our decisions. Govern our relationships. Direct our steps. Let Your unchanging Kingship be our covering, our stability, and our security. Where instability has echoed through generations, let Your eternal rule bring alignment and restoration.

Everlasting King, reign in me completely. Reign in my work, my ministry, my dreams, and my future. Your kingdom is forever—and because You reign, I will not fear. In Jesus' name, Amen.

37

Blessed Forever

> "Blessed be Yahweh, the God of Israel, from everlasting and to everlasting! Amen and amen."
> — Psalm 41:13 WEB

Devotional Insight

El Olam, the Everlasting God, invites us into praise that stretches beyond time—praise that acknowledges who He has always been and who He forever will be. This Scripture reveals a God whose worthiness does not come and go with circumstances. His goodness spans eternity. His faithfulness reaches beyond generations. When believers declare "from everlasting to everlasting," they align their hearts with the eternal nature of God's greatness. In experiences of joy or sorrow, triumph or trial, God remains worthy of blessing. As you worship the Everlasting God, you step into a divine continuity—a flow of eternal praise that strengthens your spirit and anchors your soul in His unchanging character.

Prayer

El Olam, Everlasting God, I bless Your name today with reverence and joy. From everlasting to everlasting, You are God. You deserve praise that does not fade, worship that does not waver, and honor that does not diminish with time. My heart joins the eternal chorus that has worshiped You through the ages and will continue forevermore.

Lord, teach me to bless You not only in seasons of clarity but also in seasons of mystery. Let praise rise in me that is rooted in Your eternal nature, not my temporary feelings. Open my eyes to see Your goodness woven into every detail of my journey. Remind me that You have been faithful long before I understood Your ways, and You will remain faithful long after my current situation has passed.

Let Your eternal stability rest upon my family. Establish in us a spirit of worship that outlives circumstances and withstands pressure. Let our home become a sanctuary of blessing, a place where gratitude flows naturally because we know that Your lovingkindness endures forever. Uproot every spirit of complaint, discouragement, or heaviness, and replace it with a fountain of continual praise.

El Olam, let Your everlasting presence break every cycle of fear and instability. Fill my days with reminders that You are the same God who carried previous generations and will carry the ones yet to come. Let my heart live in awe of Your eternal goodness—steady, faithful, and unending.

I bless You, Everlasting God, with all that I am, from this moment into eternity. In Jesus' name, Amen.

38

Generations in His Hands

> "Lord, you have been our dwelling place for all generations. Before the mountains were born, before you had formed the earth and the world, even from everlasting to everlasting, you are God. You turn man to destruction, saying, 'Return, you children of men.' For a thousand years in your sight are just like yesterday when it is past, like a watch in the night."
> — Psalm 90:1–4 WEB

Devotional Insight

El Olam spans generations with unbroken faithfulness. Psalm 90 reveals a God who existed before creation and remains God throughout eternity. He is the dwelling place for every generation—constant when all else changes. Time does not diminish His strength or alter His purposes. The believer finds profound peace in knowing that the same God who sustained past generations is the God who surrounds you today and the God who will guide those who come after you. His everlasting nature means your life is held within a story larger than time. You can rest in a God who is not limited by your lifespan, your challenges, or your understanding. El Olam is your dwelling place, your children's dwelling place, and your lineage's everlasting foundation.

Prayer

El Olam, Everlasting God, You have been the dwelling place of Your people throughout all generations, and today I take refuge under the shelter of Your eternal presence. Before mountains rose or oceans formed, You were God. Long after my lifetime and the lifetimes of those after me, You will still be God—unchanged, unrivaled, and forever faithful.

Lord, I thank You that my life is not left to the instability of time but held securely in the hands of the Eternal One. You see a thousand years as a single day; nothing surprises You, nothing overwhelms You, and nothing falls outside Your sovereign awareness. Teach me to rest in Your eternal perspective. Lift me out of the pressures of the moment and anchor my heart in Your everlasting timeline.

El Olam, establish Your covering over my family. You have been our dwelling place—be our refuge today and for every generation that proceeds from us. Let Your eternal presence build a heritage of faith that outlives us. Where generational fear has traveled, end it. Where generational blessings have begun, multiply them. Let Your goodness echo through my lineage as You guide each generation into Your everlasting purposes.

I release every fear tied to aging, uncertainty, or the future. You hold time, and You hold me. Return my heart again and again to the truth that I dwell in the God who cannot fade, weaken, or change. From everlasting to everlasting, You are our God.

El Olam, secure my path, my purpose, and my generations under Your eternal wings. In Jesus' name, Amen.

39

Established Forever

"Yahweh reigns! He is clothed with majesty! Yahweh is armed with strength. The world also is established. It can't be moved. Your throne is established from long ago. You are from everlasting."
— Psalm 93:1-2 WEB

Devotional Insight

El Olam reigns with eternal majesty and unending strength. His throne predates creation, and His rule secures the stability of the world. Nothing can uproot what He establishes. For the believer, this means that God's authority over your life is not temporary or fragile. He reigns over your circumstances with the same eternal strength that governs the universe. His sovereignty ensures that His purposes for you stand firm. Even when life feels unstable, God remains unmoved. El Olam's everlasting reign brings assurance that you can trust Him fully—He is clothed in majesty now just as He has been from eternity past.

Prayer

El Olam, Everlasting God, I praise You as the One who reigns in majesty. You are clothed in glory, armed with strength, and enthroned from everlasting. No throne rivals Yours. No power challenges Your sovereignty. You rule with wisdom and authority that cannot weaken or be replaced. I bow before Your eternal reign, declaring that You are Lord over my life and every season within it.

Lord, establish me with the same stability that flows from Your everlasting throne. Where my heart has been shaken, let Your strength reinforce me. Where circumstances have felt unstable, remind me that You reign above them with unbroken authority. I anchor my confidence not in what I see but in the eternal God who governs all things flawlessly.

Let Your everlasting rule cover my family. Stabilize our emotions, our finances, our relationships, and our callings. Bring order where chaos has tried to creep in. Bring strength where weakness has lingered. Bring peace where fear has spoken loudly. Let the majesty of Your reign rest upon our home, making it a place established by Your eternal presence.

El Olam, Your throne stands forever. Let every unstable foundation in my life be removed and replaced with the everlasting stability that comes from You. Teach me to rely on Your eternal strength, to worship with a heart rooted in eternity, and to walk with the assurance that Your purposes for me cannot be moved.

You are from everlasting, and I trust wholly in Your reign.
In Jesus' name, Amen.

40

Forever Faithful

"For Yahweh is good. His loving kindness endures forever, his faithfulness to all generations."
— Psalm 100:5 WEB

Devotional Insight

El Olam's everlasting nature is displayed in His enduring goodness and generational faithfulness. God's mercy does not expire; His faithfulness does not weaken; His kindness does not fluctuate with human behavior. He is eternally consistent. Every generation that turns to Him encounters the same steadfast love. For the believer, this means that God's commitment to you is not temporary—His goodness follows you, surrounds you, and upholds your lineage. You can trust Him with your future because His faithfulness extends beyond your lifetime. His love is not seasonal but eternal, rooted in His identity as the Everlasting God.

Prayer

El Olam, Everlasting God, I praise You for Your goodness that never ends and Your lovingkindness that stretches into eternity. You are faithful to all generations, and today I lean on the strength of that faithfulness. Thank You for being the God whose love does not run out, whose mercy does not shift, and whose goodness does not fade with time.

Lord, reveal the depth of Your goodness in my life. Let me see Your fingerprints in the ordinary and the extraordinary. Where I have overlooked Your kindness, open my eyes. Where I have doubted Your faithfulness, strengthen my trust. Let Your eternal lovingkindness become the stabilizing force in my days and the defining truth in my heart.

Extend Your everlasting goodness over my family. Let Your faithfulness weave through our generations. Break cycles of fear, lack, instability, or unbelief. Replace them with cycles of mercy, stability, abundance, and unwavering devotion to You. Let the testimony of our household be this: "God has been faithful, and His goodness still surrounds us."

El Olam, let Your eternal mercy heal places in me that have carried disappointment. Restore hope where it has thinned. Rekindle joy where it has dimmed. Let Your everlasting kindness cover every area of need in my life. I declare that Your goodness will not fail, Your mercy will not cease, and Your faithfulness will remain my anchor forever.

You are good, and Your lovingkindness endures forever. In Jesus' name, Amen.

41

Unchanging Through All Ages

"Of old, you laid the foundation of the earth. The heavens are the work of your hands. They will perish, but you will endure. Yes, all of them will wear out like a garment. You will change them like a cloak, and they will be changed; but you are the same. Your years will have no end. The children of your servants will continue. Their offspring will be established before you."
— Psalm 102:25–28 WEB

Devotional Insight

El Olam remains unchanged while all creation ages, shifts, and transforms. This passage reveals a God who stands unaltered through cosmic change and generational transition. Everything you see—mountains, nations, skies, even time itself—will one day fade, but God will remain forever the same. His unchanging nature becomes the foundation of stability for your life. As a believer, you rest in the eternal God whose consistency upholds your destiny and secures your lineage. El Olam assures you that His purposes for you and your family are anchored in eternity, not in the fragile conditions of the world around you.

Prayer

El Olam, Everlasting God, I worship You as the One who laid the foundation of the earth with Your own hands. All creation will one day fold like a worn-out garment, but You remain unchanged, steadfast, and eternal. While everything around me shifts, You remain my constant stability. I rest in the truth that Your years have no end, and Your nature never weakens.

Lord, steady my heart in a world that feels transient and fragile. Remind me that though circumstances may change suddenly, Your purposes for my life do not waver. You remain the same God through every season—my childhood, my present moment, and my future. Let my confidence be rooted not in what I build but in the God who cannot be shaken.

Establish my family in the everlasting strength of Your nature. Let our offspring continue before You as this Scripture promises. Surround my children and my children's children with Your eternal favor. Let Your unchanging Word shape our decisions, guide our steps, and cover our generations with stability and blessing.

El Olam, align my life with what is eternal. Deliver me from fear of change. Uproot anxiety about the future. Let the permanence of Your nature calm every storm within me. I declare that the God whose years have no end is sustaining my life, securing my foundation, and governing my destiny.

You are the same forever, and because You endure, I will endure. In Jesus' name, Amen.

42

Throne Established Forever

"As for man, his days are like grass. As a flower of the field, so he flourishes. For the wind passes over it, and it is gone. Its place remembers it no more. But Yahweh's loving kindness is from everlasting to everlasting with those who fear him, his righteousness to children's children, to those who keep his covenant, to those who remember to obey his precepts. Yahweh has established his throne in the heavens. His kingdom rules over all."

— Psalm 103:15-19 WEB

Devotional Insight

El Olam contrasts humanity's fragility with His everlasting love and righteousness. Human life fades like grass, but God's covenant mercy remains unbroken from generation to generation. His throne is established forever, and His kingdom rules over everything—time, destiny, and all creation. This everlasting nature assures the believer that while life's seasons may be brief, God's love is not. His eternal rule secures your family, your legacy, and your destiny. El Olam governs your path with unwavering covenant faithfulness, inviting you into a life anchored far beyond your earthly limitations.

Prayer

El Olam, Everlasting God, I humble myself before Your eternal throne. My days are like grass—fleeting, fragile, and easily forgotten—but Your lovingkindness stretches from everlasting to everlasting. I thank You that while my life may be temporary, Your covenant love toward me is not. Your throne is established forever, and Your kingdom rules over all things with perfect justice and unfailing mercy.

Lord, I choose to fear You with reverence and devotion. Let Your eternal righteousness flow through my life and into the generations after me. Cover my children and grandchildren with the blessing of Your everlasting kindness. Let Your covenant faithfulness shape our lineage, anchor our identity, and guide our footsteps.

Let Your eternal rule break every temporary limitation in my life. Where human weakness threatens to overwhelm me, strengthen me with the power that flows from Your everlasting kingdom. Where circumstances shift unexpectedly, remind me that Your throne is unmovable. Where I face challenges beyond my understanding, reign over them with Your sovereign authority.

El Olam, establish my heart in obedience. Let my life reflect a covenant-keeping posture—one that remembers Your Word, honors Your precepts, and walks in alignment with Your eternal purposes. Let every unstable place in my family be brought under the rule of Your everlasting kingdom.

Reign over my destiny, reign over my household, reign over my future. Your kingdom rules over all, and I rest in Your eternal dominion. In Jesus' name, Amen.

43

Mercy That Never Ends

"Praise Yahweh! Give thanks to Yahweh, for he is good, for his loving kindness endures forever."
— Psalm 106:1 WEB

Devotional Insight

El Olam reveals Himself through love that never ends and mercy that outlasts every failure and season. His goodness is constant, His kindness eternal, and His covenant love indestructible. Psalm 106:1 invites the believer into a lifestyle of thanksgiving rooted not in changing circumstances but in God's everlasting character. El Olam's enduring mercy means that every new day is met with divine compassion. His goodness is not seasonal—it is eternal, anchored in who He is. When you praise Him, you step into alignment with the eternal flow of His lovingkindness that has stretched throughout all ages and continues into your life today.

Prayer

El Olam, Everlasting God, I lift my voice in praise because Your lovingkindness endures forever. You are good—unchangeably, eternally, unfailingly good. No moment alters Your nature. No circumstance diminishes Your mercy. I bless You today for the love that met my ancestors, surrounds me now, and will continue to cover the generations after me.

Lord, let the revelation of Your everlasting mercy deepen my gratitude. Where disappointment has tried to cloud my praise, clear my vision. Where heaviness has attempted to silence my joy, lift it off by the power of Your eternal kindness. Teach me to bless You not because everything is perfect but because You are eternally good.

Let Your everlasting mercy cover my family. Heal where brokenness has lingered. Restore where loss has left wounds. Redeem where mistakes were made. Your mercy does not expire—it continues, strengthens, and revives. Let Your goodness define our story and Your compassion redirect every area of struggle.

El Olam, let my life be anchored in Your eternal kindness. Break every lie that tells me I must earn Your love. Silence every whisper that says I've exhausted Your grace. Your goodness is forever; Your mercy is limitless. I step boldly into the flow of Your everlasting lovingkindness, receiving strength, hope, and renewal for my journey.

You are good, and Your mercy endures forever—this truth will remain my song. In Jesus' name, Amen.

44

Word Forever Settled

"Yahweh, your word is settled in heaven forever. Your faithfulness is to all generations. You have established the earth, and it remains."

— Psalm 119:89–90 WEB

Devotional Insight

El Olam reveals His everlasting nature through His eternally settled Word. Nothing can alter it, weaken it, or overturn what God has spoken. His Word stands fixed in heaven, untouched by time and unaffected by change. His faithfulness flows from generation to generation, reaching into your life with the same strength it carried throughout biblical history. When you trust El Olam, you trust a God whose promises cannot fail and whose decrees cannot be undone. His eternal Word becomes your foundation, your stability, and your assurance.

Prayer

El Olam, Everlasting God, I worship You because Your Word is settled forever in heaven. Your promises are not shifting opinions; they are eternal truths. What You have spoken concerning my life is fixed, established, and unchanging. I anchor my hope in Your everlasting faithfulness, which has held generations before me and will hold generations after me.

Lord, where doubt has clouded my faith, clear it with the power of Your eternal Word. Remind me that no circumstance can contradict what You have established. Your Word is the highest authority over my life. Your promises outweigh reports, timelines, emotions, and obstacles. Let my spirit rest in what You have said, not what I see.

Let Your faithfulness cover my family. Fulfill every promise You have spoken over us. Align us with Your eternal Word—our identity, our purpose, our decisions, and our futures. Uproot every lie that contradicts Your truth. Increase our confidence in Your unchanging faithfulness.

El Olam, establish my heart with the same strength that stabilizes the earth. Where instability has attempted to shake me, let Your eternal Word fortify me. Where I have hesitated in obedience, strengthen my resolve. Let my life become a testimony of the God whose Word does not fail.

Your Word is forever settled, and Your faithfulness is forever sure. In Jesus' name, Amen.

45

Eternity Placed Within

> "He has made everything beautiful in its time. He has also set eternity in their hearts, yet no one can fathom what God has done from the beginning even to the end."
> — Ecclesiastes 3:11 WEB

Devotional Insight

El Olam not only governs eternity—He plants eternity inside the human heart. This Scripture reveals a God whose eternal purposes shape every moment and season of your life. He makes all things beautiful in their time, weaving divine intention into every process, every delay, and every unfolding chapter. While we cannot fully comprehend His eternal plan, we carry within us a longing for the everlasting—evidence of His nature stamped into our very being. To experience El Olam is to trust that your seasons are not random and your journey is not aimless. The Everlasting God is orchestrating beauty on an eternal timeline.

Prayer

El Olam, Everlasting God, I thank You for setting eternity in my heart. You have woven Your eternal nature into my being, giving me a longing for Your presence and a desire for Your purposes. You make everything beautiful in its time, and today I surrender my timetable to Your everlasting wisdom.

Lord, help me trust Your timing. Where impatience has grown, replace it with eternal perspective. Where frustration has formed, heal it with the assurance that You are working from the beginning to the end. I release every season of my life into Your hands—the waiting, the growing, the building, the pruning, the becoming. Let Your eternal plan unfold without resistance in me.

El Olam, place Your eternity-shaped vision inside my family. Let us see beyond temporary challenges and embrace Your bigger story. Make our home a place that values what is eternal over what is fleeting. Let generational purpose come alive as You align us with Your everlasting design.

Lord, beautify what has seemed barren. Restore what has felt broken. Reveal the hidden work You have been doing behind the scenes. Lead me into a deeper awareness of Your eternal presence guiding my steps and shaping my destiny.

I yield to Your eternal purposes, trusting the God who knows the beginning from the end and makes everything beautiful in His time. In Jesus' name, Amen.

46

Rock of Ages

"Trust in Yahweh forever; for in Yah, Yahweh, is an everlasting Rock."
— Isaiah 26:4 WEB

Devotional Insight

El Olam reveals Himself as the Everlasting Rock—unmoved, unbroken, and eternally dependable. This Scripture calls the believer into perpetual trust, not temporary confidence. God's everlasting nature means He remains the same through your shifting seasons, storms, and transitions. When everything else feels unstable, El Olam stands firm as your eternal foundation. Trust becomes possible not because circumstances are predictable, but because God is unchanging. His strength does not erode with time. His promises do not weaken under pressure. His character does not fluctuate with emotion. He is the Rock that supports your life, your family, and your generations forever.

Prayer

El Olam, Everlasting God, I place my trust in You with fresh surrender. You are my eternal Rock—unyielding, unshakable, and unwavering in strength. You are my stability in every season. When the winds of life rise and the ground beneath me shifts, You remain the foundation that cannot be moved. I anchor my heart to You alone.

Lord, teach me to trust You forever—not only in moments of clarity but in moments of uncertainty. Let my confidence in You transcend my feelings, circumstances, and understanding. Where fear has tried to unsettle me, let the revelation of Your everlasting strength bring peace. Where doubt has whispered lies, let Your eternal truth silence every voice contrary to Your Word.

Establish my family upon the Rock of Ages. Let our home be built on a foundation that cannot crack beneath pressure. Strengthen our faith, our unity, our resilience, and our devotion to You. Break every unstable pattern and replace it with the solidity of Your everlasting nature.

El Olam, where I have leaned on temporary supports, shift my dependence to You. Become the Rock of my decisions, the Rock of my emotions, the Rock of my future. Let everything built on Your eternal strength flourish, and let everything not anchored in You fall away.

I trust You forever, my Everlasting Rock. In Jesus' name, Amen.

47

Strength Without Weariness

"Haven't you known? Haven't you heard? The everlasting God, Yahweh, the Creator of the ends of the earth, doesn't faint. He isn't weary. His understanding is unsearchable."
— Isaiah 40:28 WEB

Devotional Insight

El Olam is the Everlasting God whose strength never diminishes and whose understanding cannot be exhausted. Unlike human endurance, God's power does not decline, and His wisdom does not reach limits. This Scripture invites believers to rest in the One who never grows tired of sustaining them, guiding them, or fighting for them. When your strength collapses, His remains. When your understanding ends, His begins. El Olam carries you, empowers you, renews you, and surrounds you with tireless love. You can rely on Him without fear that He will ever weaken or withdraw.

Prayer

El Olam, Everlasting God, I exalt You as the Creator who never grows weary. You hold the ends of the earth in Your hands, and yet You hold me with tender strength. You do not faint in Your care for me, nor do You weaken in Your watchfulness. Your energy is infinite, Your power unfailing, and Your wisdom unsearchable. I rest in the truth that I serve a God who never tires of sustaining my life.

Lord, renew my strength where I have felt drained. Lift me where I have fallen under pressure. Restore my joy where fatigue has settled into my soul. You are the God who does not grow weary—and because I belong to You, I receive the strength that flows from Your everlasting nature.

Let Your infinite understanding guide my decisions. Where I lack clarity, illuminate my path. Where confusion has clouded my mind, replace it with divine perspective. Lead my family with Your unsearchable wisdom and bring order to every area that feels overwhelming.

El Olam, sustain my household with tireless grace. Carry us through every season that demands more than we possess. Strengthen marriages, empower parents, encourage children, and revive every weary heart under our roof. Let Your everlasting energy rejuvenate our spirits.

I surrender my exhaustion, confusion, and limitations into Your eternal hands. You are the God who never faints, never falters, and never fails. In Jesus' name, Amen.

48

The God Who Declares the End

> "Remember the former things of old: for I am God, and there is no other. I am God, and there is none like me, declaring the end from the beginning, and from ancient times things that are not yet done, saying: 'My counsel will stand, and I will do all that I please.'"
> — Isaiah 46:9–10 WEB

Devotional Insight

El Olam, the Everlasting God, governs time with sovereign authority. This Scripture reveals a God who knows the end before the beginning begins. His counsel stands unmoved by circumstances, opposition, or delay. For the believer, this means your life is not unfolding randomly—God has already established the outcome. His eternal purposes are not threatened by human limitation or spiritual resistance. He does not react; He ordains. And because He is everlasting, nothing can interrupt or overturn what He has declared. El Olam invites you to trust that the God who wrote your story from eternity will fulfill every promise He designed for you.

Prayer

El Olam, Everlasting God, I honor You as the One who declares the end from the beginning. There is none like You—no power, no wisdom, no force can rival Your sovereignty. You see what I cannot. You know what I have yet to experience. You orchestrate every detail with eternal precision. I yield my life into the hands of the God who has already established my victory.

Lord, let Your eternal counsel stand over my life. Where the enemy has tried to impose fear, remind me that Your decree is final. Where I have doubted Your timing, strengthen my trust in Your eternal plan. You declared my destiny long before I faced my challenges. You established my purpose before I encountered resistance. I choose to align my heart with what You have spoken—not what I feel.

Establish Your purposes in my family. Reveal the destiny You formed for our generations. Let every contrary voice be silenced by Your eternal Word. Let every delay bow to Your divine timing. Let every opposition crumble under Your everlasting counsel.

El Olam, do all that You please in my life. I surrender my timelines, my expectations, and my anxieties. You are the God who began the work and the God who will bring it to completion. Nothing can interrupt Your purposes.

Your counsel will stand—over my path, my home, my calling, and my generations. In Jesus' name, Amen.

49

Majesty of Eternity

"For the high and lofty One who inhabits eternity, whose name is Holy, says: 'I dwell in the high and holy place, with him also who is of a contrite and humble spirit, to revive the spirit of the humble, and to revive the heart of the contrite.'"
— Isaiah 57:15 WEB

Devotional Insight

El Olam is the God who inhabits eternity—yet He draws near to the humble. His transcendence does not create distance but becomes the foundation of His compassion. He dwells in heights beyond comprehension, yet He also dwells with those whose hearts are bowed before Him. His eternal nature releases revival, renewal, and restoration into the spirits of those who yield to Him. You experience El Olam not only as the unreachable God of eternity but as the intimate God who revives the broken and strengthens the contrite. Eternity meets humanity in His presence.

Prayer

El Olam, Everlasting God, You inhabit eternity, and yet You come close to me. You are high and lifted up, dwelling in unapproachable light, but You also dwell with the humble and contrite. I bow before Your holiness with reverence and gratitude. Thank You for choosing to revive my spirit and restore my heart.

Lord, let humility mark my life. Strip away pride, self-reliance, and every barrier that keeps me from experiencing Your nearness. I want to dwell with the God who inhabits eternity. Revive my weary heart. Breathe new life into places within me that have grown tired, discouraged, or wounded. Let the eternal God release fresh strength into my soul.

Extend revival into my family. Let Your presence dwell among us—reviving every discouraged heart, healing every broken place, and restoring every weary soul. Teach us to walk humbly, to depend fully on You, and to welcome the nearness of the God who spans eternity.

El Olam, inhabit every room of my home. Saturate us with Your holiness. Let eternity shape our priorities, soften our hearts, and direct our steps. Bring fresh renewal where routine has dulled our passion. Bring revival where heaviness has lingered. Bring restoration where hope has thinned.

You are the high and lofty One—and You dwell with me. Thank You for Your nearness, Your compassion, and Your eternal presence. In Jesus' name, Amen.

50

Everlasting Love

"Yahweh appeared of old to me, saying, 'Yes, I have loved you with an everlasting love. Therefore I have drawn you with loving kindness.'"

— Jeremiah 31:3 WEB

Devotional Insight

El Olam's eternal nature is expressed through everlasting love—a love without beginning or end, a love that does not shift with behavior, seasons, or circumstances. God's love is not reactive; it is rooted in eternity. He draws His people with kindness that originates in His eternal heart. For the believer, this means your worth, security, and identity are grounded in a love that cannot fade, break, or expire. The Everlasting God loves you with an unending affection that stretches across time, into your past, through your present, and into your future. His love is your anchor.

Prayer

El Olam, Everlasting God, I receive Your everlasting love with humility and awe. You have loved me with a love that predates my existence and will outlast every circumstance of my life. Your lovingkindness draws me, comforts me, heals me, and surrounds me. I rest in the assurance that Your love is not temporary—it is eternal.

Lord, let the revelation of Your everlasting love heal every wounded place within me. Where rejection has left scars, cover them with Your eternal acceptance. Where fear has taken root, uproot it with the security of Your unfailing affection. Where shame has lingered, wash it away with the truth that Your love has no end.

Let Your everlasting love permeate my family. Surround my household with Your kindness. Heal relationships, restore communication, and break cycles of emotional pain. Let the atmosphere of our home be shaped by the God whose love is eternal and whose kindness continually draws us closer.

El Olam, anchor my identity in Your love. Let me see myself through the lens of Your eternal affection, not through the opinions or actions of others. Strengthen my confidence, deepen my peace, and align my heart with the truth that I am eternally loved by an eternal God.

Draw me daily with Your lovingkindness. Lead me deeper into fellowship with You. Surround me with Your everlasting presence. In Jesus' name, Amen.

51

Reigning Forever

"You, Yahweh, remain forever. Your throne is from generation to generation."
— Lamentations 5:19 WEB

Devotional Insight

El Olam stands enthroned across generations, unchanged by time or turmoil. While earthly kingdoms rise and fall, the throne of God remains forever secure. This Scripture reminds the believer that God's rule is not temporary or vulnerable; His sovereignty stretches across every age and season. When you face instability, loss, or sorrow, El Olam invites you to lift your eyes to His eternal throne—a place untouched by decay, defeat, or disruption. His reign anchors your family, your purpose, and your future. You can trust Him fully because His authority never diminishes and His presence never fades.

Prayer

El Olam, Everlasting God, I lift my eyes to Your eternal throne. You remain forever—unchanged, unshaken, and unmoved by the passing of time. While everything around me shifts, Your throne endures from generation to generation. I take refuge in the permanence of Your reign and in the certainty of Your dominion.

Lord, rule over every area of my life. Let Your sovereignty govern my decisions, calm my fears, and stabilize my heart. Where sorrow has lingered, bring comfort. Where grief has weighed heavily, bring renewal. Remind me that no darkness, no loss, and no season can dethrone the God who reigns forever.

Let Your eternal rule rest upon my family. Establish our home under Your authority and let Your presence govern our generations. Bring alignment to every misaligned place. Bring order where confusion has entered. Bring peace where turmoil has tried to reign. Let our lineage be marked by the blessing of a household under the rule of the Eternal King.

Lord, I surrender every throne I have tried to build for myself—thrones of control, self-reliance, or fear. Take Your rightful place as ruler of my heart, my home, and my destiny. Teach me to walk in reverence of the God who reigns without interruption or expiration.

El Olam, Your throne stands forever. I rest in Your reign today and for all generations to come. In Jesus' name, Amen.

52

King of Heaven Forever

> "At the end of the days I, Nebuchadnezzar, lifted up my eyes to heaven, and my understanding returned to me; and I blessed the Most High, and I praised and honored him who lives forever; for his dominion is an everlasting dominion, and his kingdom from generation to generation."
> — Daniel 4:34 WEB

Devotional Insight

El Olam is the God who lives forever, whose dominion is eternal, whose kingdom stretches beyond time. Even kings must bow to Him. When human pride crumbles and worldly power fails, the everlasting rule of God remains. This Scripture reveals that understanding and clarity return when eyes are lifted toward the Eternal God. His dominion outlasts all earthly authority, and His kingdom is not governed by human timelines. For the believer, this means no force—political, spiritual, economic, or emotional—can overthrow the God who reigns forever. El Olam anchors your identity and future in a kingdom that cannot be shaken.

Prayer

El Olam, Everlasting God, I lift my eyes to You, the One who lives forever. You reign with eternal dominion. Your kingdom endures from generation to generation. You are unchallenged, unrivaled, and unstoppable. I bless Your holy name, declaring that no earthly power compares to Your eternal rule.

Lord, restore understanding and clarity to me as I look toward You. Where confusion has clouded my mind, lift it. Where pride has blinded me, humble me. Where fear has overshadowed my decisions, replace it with faith. Let the revelation of Your everlasting kingdom reset my perspective and align my heart with Your eternal purposes.

Let Your kingdom rule be established in my family. Let every generational stronghold bow to Your dominion. Let every form of pride, rebellion, or oppression fall under the authority of the everlasting King. Let Your righteousness, peace, and joy permeate every area of our household.

El Olam, let Your eternal dominion govern my future. I refuse to fear what is temporary when I belong to a kingdom that is everlasting. Strengthen my faith in seasons of uncertainty. Remind me that You reign above every circumstance, every authority, and every challenge.

I honor You, Most High God, who lives forever. Your kingdom is my refuge. Your rule is my security. Your dominion is my peace. In Jesus' name, Amen.

53

Ancient of Days, Unmoving

> "He stood, and shook the earth. He looked, and made the nations tremble. The ancient mountains were scattered. The age-old hills collapsed. His ways are eternal."
> — Habakkuk 3:6 WEB

Devotional Insight

El Olam's ways are eternal—unbounded by time, unchanged by circumstance, unstoppable in power. This Scripture paints a picture of the Everlasting God whose presence shakes the earth and humbles nations. Even ancient mountains dissolve before Him, yet His purposes remain unshaken. For the believer, the eternal ways of God become the foundation of hope. He is not learning as He goes; He is not adjusting plans in reaction. His ways are established in eternity and are perfect, victorious, and unstoppable. You can trust that the God whose ways are eternal is guiding you with wisdom older than the world itself.

Prayer

El Olam, Everlasting God, I stand in awe of Your eternal ways. When You rise, the earth trembles. When You look, nations shake. Mountains that seem immovable crumble before You, yet You remain forever unchanging. Your ways are eternal, and I surrender to their wisdom, power, and perfection.

Lord, shake everything in my life that needs to be shaken. Scatter every obstacle that stands against Your purpose. Collapse every ancient stronghold—seen or unseen—that has resisted Your will in my family. Let nothing stand tall where You have decreed that it must fall. Make Your eternal ways visible in my life.

Bring stability where my heart has felt shaken. Bring clarity where confusion has tried to linger. Bring courage where fear has taken root. You are the God whose ways stretch beyond time, and I trust what You are doing even when I cannot yet see the outcome.

El Olam, establish Your eternal ways in my household. Let Your purposes override every generational pattern that opposes Your will. Bring transformation that only the Ancient of Days can initiate. Guide us according to wisdom that predates creation and love that outlasts eternity.

Your eternal ways are my security. Your everlasting nature is my confidence. Lead me deeper into alignment with Your timeless purposes. In Jesus' name, Amen.

54

The Eternal God Revealed

> "But now has been revealed, and by the Scriptures of the prophets, according to the commandment of the eternal God, made known for all the obedience of faith."
> — Romans 16:26 WEB

Devotional Insight

El Olam reveals His eternal purposes through His Word and by His command. What was hidden is now made known—not by human reasoning, but by divine revelation. The eternal God unveils His will so that His people can walk in obedience rooted in faith. His purposes are ancient yet freshly revealed. His commandments are eternal yet powerfully active in your present life. When you encounter El Olam, you receive insight that aligns you with His timeless wisdom and empowers you to live in obedience that produces blessing and destiny fulfillment.

Prayer

El Olam, Eternal God, I bless You for revealing Your purposes to me. You are not silent, distant, or hidden. You unveil Your will through Your Word, by Your Spirit, and through Your prophetic Scriptures. I honor You as the God whose eternal purposes now shine into my life with clarity and grace.

Lord, align me with the obedience of faith. Let every revelation You release produce transformation in me. Remove stubbornness, doubt, and hesitation. Let my heart respond quickly and joyfully to Your eternal commands. As You reveal Your will, empower me to walk in it with courage and conviction.

Make Your eternal purposes known in my family. Illuminate our path. Break confusion. Silence every misleading voice. Let the eternal God direct our decisions, our stewardship, our relationships, and our future. Transform our home into a place where revelation flows freely and obedience is embraced joyfully.

El Olam, let what You have commanded stand firm in my life. Let no distraction, fear, or delay hinder my obedience. Let every promise You have revealed begin to manifest. Let every instruction You have given become fruitful through obedience.

You are the Eternal God who reveals, commands, directs, and fulfills. I surrender to Your timeless wisdom and embrace the obedience of faith. In Jesus' name, Amen.

55

Immortal Majesty

> "Now to the King eternal, immortal, invisible, the only God, be honor and glory forever and ever. Amen."
> — 1 Timothy 1:17 WEB

Devotional Insight

El Olam is the King eternal—immortal, invisible, unmatched in glory and deserving of endless honor. This Scripture positions the believer in worship before the majesty of a God who cannot die, cannot decay, cannot diminish. His eternal kingship invites you into a life anchored in His permanence rather than the fragility of worldly systems. When you worship the Eternal King, your perspective shifts. You see your challenges through the lens of God's immortality and your future through the lens of His everlasting dominion. El Olam reigns forever, and His glory shapes the destiny of His people.

Prayer

El Olam, King eternal, immortal, invisible, the only wise God, I bow before Your majesty. You alone deserve honor and glory forever. No throne compares to Yours. No kingdom rivals the power of Your reign. You exist beyond time, beyond decay, beyond limitation. I worship You with reverence and awe.

Lord, let my life reflect the honor due to the Eternal King. Purify my thoughts, align my desires, and shape my actions so that they bring glory to Your name. Let no idol occupy the place reserved for You alone. Let no fear overshadow the authority of the immortal God who rules over my life.

Reign over my family with eternal dominion. Establish Your glory in our home. Let Your presence fill the atmosphere, bringing purity, peace, and divine order. Remove anything that dishonors Your name. Let our household reflect the majesty of the God we serve.

El Olam, shift my perspective from the temporary to the eternal. Let me live with the assurance that the immortal God is guiding my steps. Let me face challenges with the confidence that nothing can outlive or overpower You. Let me dream boldly, pray boldly, and obey boldly because Your reign is forever.

To the King eternal, immortal, invisible—the only God—be honor and glory through my life, my family, and my generations. In Jesus' name, Amen.

56

Eternal Spirit

"How much more will the blood of Christ, who through the eternal Spirit offered himself without defect to God, cleanse your conscience from dead works to serve the living God?"
— Hebrews 9:14 WEB

Devotional Insight

El Olam reveals Himself through the eternal Spirit, the One who empowered Christ's perfect offering and who continues to work within believers today. The Spirit is not limited by time—He cleanses, renews, and transforms across generations. This Scripture shows that the blood of Christ, applied by the eternal Spirit, reaches into the deepest parts of a believer's conscience, freeing them from cycles of guilt and lifeless striving. El Olam's eternal nature means His work in you is not temporary but lasting, powerful, and ongoing. He purifies the heart so you may serve God in true freedom.

Prayer

El Olam, Everlasting God, I worship You as the One who works through the eternal Spirit. Thank You for the blood of Christ that cleanses my conscience and removes every stain of guilt from my past. Thank You for the Spirit who never grows weary, never weakens, and never stops perfecting the work of holiness within me.

Lord, cleanse me deeply today. Remove every dead work—every self-reliant attempt to earn what Christ has already purchased. Purify my motives, renew my desires, and awaken my spirit to serve the living God with joy, passion, and reverence. Let the eternal Spirit breathe life into every dormant place within me.

Let Your eternal cleansing flow through my family. Heal wounded consciences, restore broken confidence, and break patterns of guilt, shame, and striving. Let the blood of Christ applied by the eternal Spirit mark our household with freedom, purity, and renewed purpose.

El Olam, let the work You begin in us continue with everlasting force. Carry us from dead works into living worship. Let Your Spirit empower our obedience, our prayers, our decisions, and our relationships. Make us vessels fit for Your glory.

I surrender to the cleansing of the eternal Spirit and the everlasting love that makes me whole. In Jesus' name, Amen.

57

Forever the Same

> "Jesus Christ is the same yesterday, today, and forever."
> — Hebrews 13:8 WEB

Devotional Insight

El Olam is fully revealed in Christ, the One who embodies eternal consistency. Jesus does not change in compassion, power, truth, or purpose. The same Jesus who healed, delivered, forgave, restored, and resurrected continues His work in believers today. His nature does not evolve or diminish with time. He is the eternal Christ whose faithfulness stretches beyond the past into the present and the future. For the believer, this means you can trust His Word, His character, and His promises without fear that He will ever shift. The everlasting God made visible in Christ is your unchanging anchor.

Prayer

Lord Jesus, Eternal Christ, I worship You as the One who remains the same yesterday, today, and forever. You are immutable in love, steadfast in strength, and unwavering in power. I rest in the truth that the Jesus who moved mightily through Scripture is the same Jesus moving in my life right now.

Lord, strengthen my faith in Your unchanging nature. Where fear has whispered that Your promises will fail, silence it with the certainty of who You are. Where doubt has clouded my vision, restore clarity. Where discouragement has weighed on my heart, lift it with the assurance that You have not changed.

Let Your unchanging presence fill my home. Jesus, reign over my family with the same authority You demonstrated on earth. Heal those who are hurting, restore those who feel broken, uplift those who feel weary, and guide those who feel uncertain. Let our household experience the eternal Christ in fresh and powerful ways.

Lord, establish my future in the confidence of Your unchanging Word. Align my decisions with Your eternal wisdom. Lead me into everything You intended before time began. Let my life reflect the power of a Savior who does not shift with seasons or circumstances.

You are forever the same—faithful, mighty, merciful, holy, and good. I place my trust completely in You.

In Your name I pray, Amen.

58

The Word That Lives Forever

> "For, 'All flesh is like grass, and all of man's glory like the flower of the grass. The grass withers, and its flower falls; but the Lord's word endures forever.' This is the word of Good News which was preached to you."
> — 1 Peter 1:24–25 WEB

Devotional Insight

El Olam expresses His eternal nature through His everlasting Word. Human strength fades, achievements wither, and earthly glory collapses, but God's Word remains unbroken and eternal. This Scripture reminds believers that everything temporary must bow to the eternal truth of God. His promises outlast seasons, emotions, setbacks, and circumstances. The Good News itself is not dated—it carries everlasting power to transform lives. When you anchor your life to the Word of the Everlasting God, you stand on a foundation that cannot decay.

Prayer

El Olam, Everlasting God, I honor You for Your Word that endures forever. Everything around me is temporary—my emotions, my circumstances, my challenges—but Your Word stands eternal. Thank You for the Good News that is unchanging, uncorrupted, and eternally powerful.

Lord, let Your eternal Word take root in my heart. Where I have relied on my own strength, shift my trust back to Your promises. Where I have been impressed by the fading glory of people, redirect my awe to the permanence of Your truth. Let every decision I make flow from the foundation of Your everlasting Word.

Strengthen my family with the power of Scripture. Let Your Word shape our values, anchor our identity, and secure our destiny. Remove every lie planted in our hearts. Replace them with the truth that lives forever. Let Scripture become the guiding voice in our home and the light that leads every generation forward.

El Olam, teach me to stand firm when life shifts. Let Your eternal Word silence fear, break anxiety, and uproot confusion. Let every promise You have spoken over me flourish with the strength of eternity behind it.

Your Word will endure forever—and so will every promise You have declared concerning me. In Jesus' name, Amen.

59

The God Who Is, Was, and Is to Come

"John to the seven assemblies that are in Asia: Grace to you and peace from God, who is and who was and who is to come; and from the seven Spirits who are before his throne."
— Revelation 1:4 WEB

Devotional Insight

El Olam spans all dimensions of time—past, present, and future. He is the God who is, who was, and who is to come. Nothing escapes His eternal presence. He stands in your yesterday, walks with you today, and waits for you in your tomorrow. His grace and peace flow from His eternal nature, supplying what you need in every season. This Scripture reveals that the Everlasting God is active in your life across all timelines, orchestrating purpose, providing peace, and sustaining you with eternal grace. In Him, nothing is uncertain.

Prayer

El Olam, Everlasting God, I worship You as the One who is, who was, and who is to come. You stand beyond time yet enter every moment of my life with grace and peace. Your eternal presence surrounds me—behind me, before me, and within me. I take comfort in knowing that my past is covered, my present is guided, and my future is secured by the God who spans all ages.

Lord, release Your eternal grace over every area of my life. Let Your peace settle deep in my spirit. Calm every storm, quiet every fear, and strengthen every weak place. Fill me with confidence that Your everlasting nature governs my steps.

Cover my family with the God who is and was and is to come. Heal our past wounds with Your eternal compassion. Guide our present with Your wisdom. Secure our future with Your unchanging promises. Let Your peace be the atmosphere of our home and Your grace the foundation of our decisions.

El Olam, align my heart with Your eternal timeline. Remove anxiety about the future. Heal regret from the past. Draw me into the stillness of Your peace in the present moment. Let Your everlasting nature redefine how I see every season of my life.

You are the Eternal God, faithful in every moment, and I rest in You. In Jesus' name, Amen.

60

The Living One Forever

"I am he who lives, and was dead, and behold, I am alive forevermore. Amen. I have the keys of Death and of Hades."
— Revelation 1:18 WEB

Devotional Insight

El Olam is revealed fully in the resurrected Christ, the One who conquered death and lives forever. His eternal life is not symbolic—He truly lives, reigns, and holds absolute authority over death and every realm of darkness. This Scripture assures believers that the Everlasting God is not distant but victorious, powerful, and actively ruling. When Christ holds the keys, no prison—emotional, spiritual, or generational—can remain locked. His eternal life guarantees your freedom, your victory, and your destiny. You belong to the God who lives forever.

Prayer

Lord Jesus, Eternal Living One, I worship You. You were dead, but now You live forevermore. You hold the keys of Death and Hades, and Your victory is final, unshakeable, and everlasting. I exalt You as the resurrected King whose life conquers every form of darkness.

Lord, let Your eternal life flow into every area of mine. Where hope has died, resurrect it. Where joy has faded, revive it. Where dreams have been buried, breathe life into them again. Let Your everlasting victory break every chain that has held me captive. No power of darkness can override the authority of the One who holds the keys.

Extend Your resurrection power into my family. Break generational cycles, destroy every form of spiritual oppression, and unlock every door that has been shut. Let Your eternal life govern our atmosphere, our decisions, our relationships, and our future.

El Olam, Living One, give me boldness to walk in the victory You purchased. Remove fear, silence intimidation, and strengthen my spirit. Let me live with the assurance that the eternal Christ walks with me, fights for me, and reigns over my path.

You live forevermore—and because You live, I will live. Because You hold the keys, no darkness can bind me. Because You reign, my destiny is secure.

I honor You, Eternal Living King. In Jesus' name, Amen.

PRAYERSCRIPTS
Speaking God's Word Back to Him

The Supreme God

◇

אֵל רֳאִי

EL ROI
The God Who Sees Me

Prayers to Trust the God Who Knows and Watches Over You

CYRIL OPOKU

Preface to Book 7

> "Those who know your name will put their trust in you, for you, Yahweh, have not forsaken those who seek you."
> — Psalms 9:10 (WEB)

Trust is born where awareness meets assurance, and Psalm 9:10 reveals that those who truly *know* God's Name discover a confidence that cannot be shaken. This promise anchors Book 7—*EL ROI: The God Who Sees Me*. To know God as **El Roi** is to trust Him in the most personal and vulnerable places of life—the unseen moments, the overlooked seasons, and the quiet struggles that never make it into words. El Roi is the God who sees not only actions, but hearts; not only outcomes, but journeys; not only crowds, but individuals.

The Name El Roi first emerges in a moment of deep distress, when Hagar—alone, displaced, and misunderstood—encounters God in the wilderness. In that encounter, she discovers a breathtaking truth: the God of heaven sees her. This revelation transforms despair into hope and abandonment into assurance. Psalm 9:10 echoes this same reality generations later, affirming that God has never forsaken those who seek Him. El Roi is the living proof of that promise. His sight is not passive observation; it is attentive, compassionate, and responsive. He sees in order to care. He notices in order to act.

This book invites you to trust God in places where you may feel invisible, forgotten, or misunderstood. El Roi sees the prayers you struggle to articulate, the burdens you carry quietly, and the faith you cling to when answers feel distant. As you move through these prayers, may the knowledge of His seeing bring healing to hidden wounds and confidence to weary hearts. You are not unseen. You are not overlooked. You are not forsaken. To know His Name is to rest in the assurance that the God who sees you also walks with you—faithfully, tenderly, and without fail.

To the Praise of His Name!

Cyril O.

(Illinois | December 2025)

Introduction to Book 7

Have you ever wondered if God truly sees what you're going through when no one else seems to notice?

EL ROI: *The God Who Sees Me* invites you into one of the most intimate revelations of God's nature—the assurance that He is deeply aware of your life, your struggles, and your story. El Roi is the God who sees you in the wilderness seasons, the hidden battles, and the moments when you feel overlooked or forgotten. His seeing is not distant or detached; it is personal, compassionate, and purposeful. When you know God as El Roi, trust grows—not because circumstances immediately change, but because you are no longer alone within them.

This volume is part of **Part 1 (Books 1–8)** of *The Supreme God* series, following the revelations of Elohim, Yahweh, Adonai, El Elyon, El Shaddai, and El Olam. You are encouraged to continue through the remaining book in Part 1—El Gibbor—before entering **Part 2 (Books 9–16)**, where God's glory, truth, knowledge, holiness, life, heavenly authority, and kingship are revealed in greater depth. Together, the series forms a rich and holistic portrait of the God who desires to be known.

As you begin this book, may you encounter El Roi not just as a truth to believe, but as a presence to experience—the God who sees you fully and loves you completely.

61

The God Who Finds Me

"Yahweh's angel found her by a fountain of water in the wilderness, by the fountain on the way to Shur. He said, 'Hagar, Sarai's servant, where did you come from? Where are you going?' She said, 'I am fleeing from the face of my mistress Sarai.' Yahweh's angel said to her, 'Return to your mistress, and submit yourself under her hands.' Yahweh's angel said to her, 'I will greatly multiply your offspring, that they will not be counted for multitude.' Yahweh's angel said to her, 'Behold, you are with child, and will bear a son. You shall call his name Ishmael, because Yahweh has heard your affliction. He will be like a wild donkey among men. His hand will be against every man, and every man's hand against him. He will live opposite all of his brothers.' She called the name of Yahweh who spoke to her, 'You are a God who sees,' for she said, 'Have I even stayed alive after seeing him?'"
— Genesis 16:7–13 WEB

Devotional Insight

El Roi meets us in the wilderness seasons—the places where we feel unseen, unheard, and overwhelmed. Hagar discovered that God not only knew her name but also her story, her fears, and her future. El Roi is the God who sees you in your distress and speaks purpose into moments that feel empty or chaotic. His seeing is not passive observation; it is active intervention, guidance, compassion, and promise. He sees the tears you never voiced and the questions you never dared to ask. This Scripture reminds the believer that even when you are running, God is pursuing. Even when you feel lost, He knows the way forward. El Roi reveals Himself as both the One who searches and the One who stays. In Him, you find comfort, dignity restored, calling revived, and hope reignited. He is the God who sees *you*—not generically, but personally and lovingly.

Prayer

El Roi, God who sees me, I lift my heart before You with awe and gratitude. You are the God who finds me in the hidden places, the silent pain, the wildernesses I never meant to enter. You locate me even when I cannot locate myself, and You call me by name when others only call my mistakes. Thank You for being the God who searches me out with compassion instead of condemnation.

Father, I invite Your seeing into every corner of my life—my wounds, my regrets, my unspoken fears, my weary hopes. Let Your gaze bring healing where I have carried shame, restoration where I have felt forgotten, and clarity where confusion has clouded my path. As You met Hagar and spoke promise to her, speak purpose over me and my family. Let every wilderness become a meeting place with El Roi.

Lord, reveal the next steps before me. When I am tempted to flee from hardship, help me hear Your gentle command leading me into paths of peace, growth, and destiny. May Your vision redefine my identity so I no longer live from wounds but from the Word You have spoken.

El Roi, watch over my home, my loved ones, my journey, and my future. Lift my eyes to see that I am never abandoned. Surround me with Your assurance that Your plans for me are still alive, expanding, and unstoppable. Where I feel unseen, let Your presence become my anchor.

I declare that every season of hiding is shifting into a season of divine visibility—not for human applause, but for holy alignment. God who sees me, establish me in Your promise, strengthen me in Your presence, and steady me under Your watchful care. In Jesus' name, Amen.

62

Kept in His Watchful Presence

> "Behold, I am with you, and will keep you, wherever you go, and will bring you again into this land; for I will not leave you, until I have done that which I have spoken of to you."
> — Genesis 28:15 WEB

Devotional Insight

El Roi is not only the God who sees where you are—He is the God who goes with you wherever life takes you. Jacob was running, afraid, uncertain, and alone, yet God met him with a covenant promise of continual presence and protection. The everlasting God who sees is also the faithful God who keeps. His watchful eye is paired with His keeping hand, ensuring that no journey is too far, no situation too complex, and no distance too great for His care. For the believer today, this means God is actively involved in your path—guiding, shielding, redirecting, and completing His plans in your life. El Roi is not distant; He is intimately engaged, committed to finishing what He started in you. You are never outside His line of sight and never outside His covenant grip.

Prayer

O El Roi, my Keeper and my Companion, thank You for the promise that You are with me and will keep me wherever I go. Your presence is my true security. Your watchful eye is my assurance. Your covenant faithfulness steadies my steps. I surrender my journey into Your hands, trusting that no part of my path escapes Your divine attention.

Lord, go before me into every decision, every transition, every responsibility, and every unknown season. Keep me aligned with Your will. Keep my family sheltered beneath Your wings. Keep my heart from wandering and my thoughts from straying into fear. As You vowed never to leave Jacob until Your word was fulfilled, let Your promise stand firm over my life.

Father, complete the things You have spoken concerning me. Bring me into the land of Your intentions—into purpose, provision, strength, and spiritual maturity. Where I have doubted my direction, let Your seeing and keeping correct my course. Where I have feared being left behind, reassure me with Your unfailing nearness.

El Roi, surround my household with Your vigilant presence. Let Your keeping power shield us from danger, deception, and distraction. Let Your favor follow us, and let Your wisdom guide us. Bring to pass every promise spoken over my destiny, and let no opposition derail the work of Your hands.

I declare that I walk under divine supervision and divine companionship. I will not be abandoned, not overlooked, not forgotten. The God who sees me is the God who keeps me, and His word over my life will stand. In Jesus' name, Amen.

63

The God Who Remembers My Cry

"After many days, the king of Egypt died, and the children of Israel sighed because of the bondage, and they cried, and their cry came up to God because of the bondage. God heard their groaning, and God remembered his covenant with Abraham, with Isaac, and with Jacob. God saw the children of Israel, and God understood."
— Exodus 2:23–25 WEB

Devotional Insight

El Roi is the God who sees your suffering and refuses to ignore your cry. Israel's groaning was not eloquent; it was raw, weary, and wordless, yet God received it as prayer. He saw their affliction, heard their pain, remembered His covenant, and moved to act. For the believer today, this reveals a God who is deeply attentive—One who hears even the prayers you cannot articulate and understands burdens you cannot explain. His seeing leads to compassion, and His compassion leads to intervention. El Roi is not distant from your bondage, battles, or burdens; He is near, remembering every promise spoken over your life. His seeing brings hope that no suffering is wasted and no cry is lost.

Prayer

El Roi, God who sees and understands, I come before You with every groan of my heart—spoken and unspoken. Thank You for being the God who listens when I cannot form words, who understands the depth of my pain, and who remembers every promise concerning me and my family.

Lord, gaze upon every area of bondage, limitation, and hardship in my life. See my weariness, my battles, and my hidden struggles. Let Your covenant compassion arise on my behalf. Just as You moved toward Israel when their cries reached heaven, move toward me with deliverance, breakthrough, and undeniable intervention.

Father, remember Your promises over my household. Remember the prayers I have prayed, the seeds I have sown, the hopes I have held onto. Let nothing You intended for me be stolen, delayed, or denied. Step into my circumstances with Your mighty power, bringing freedom where oppression has lingered and clarity where confusion has taken root.

God who understands, comfort my heart where I have felt misunderstood by others. Interpret my tears. Translate my groans. Let the assurance of Your seeing become the healing of my soul. Surround my family with Your mercy, lifting every burden and breaking every chain.

I declare that my cry is not forgotten. My pain is not invisible. My future is not abandoned. El Roi is rising in my life to bring deliverance, restoration, and covenant fulfillment. In Jesus' name, Amen.

64

Seen in My Affliction

> "Yahweh said, 'I have surely seen the affliction of my people who are in Egypt, and have heard their cry because of their taskmasters; for I know their sorrows. I have come down to deliver them out of the hand of the Egyptians, and to bring them up out of that land to a good and large land, to a land flowing with milk and honey...'"
> — Exodus 3:7–8 WEB

Devotional Insight

El Roi is the God who sees not only your location but also your affliction. He does not overlook your burdens or minimize your pain. The same God who saw Israel's suffering sees yours with perfect clarity and heartfelt compassion. His seeing moves Him to come down—to intervene personally, powerfully, and redemptively. For the believer, this Scripture reveals a God who is not simply aware of your struggles but actively present to deliver, restore, and reposition you into a place of promise. El Roi sees your sorrow, knows your history, and prepares your future. You are never abandoned in suffering; God is stepping toward you with deliverance.

Prayer

El Roi, the God who sees my affliction, I stand before You with reverence and hope. Thank You for seeing my struggles, my frustrations, and the silent battles I fight. Thank You that none of my pain is hidden from You and none of my tears fall unnoticed.

Lord, as You declared that You have surely seen the affliction of Your people, let Your eyes be upon my home and my journey. Look upon every hardship, injustice, and spiritual assault against my life. Hear the cry of my heart, and let Your compassion rise to intervene. Come down, O Lord, and deliver me from every bondage—physical, emotional, financial, or spiritual—that seeks to hold me captive.

Father, bring me out of every tight place and into the spacious land of Your promise. Lead me into rest where there has been toil, abundance where there has been lack, and joy where there has been sorrow. Let Your presence escort me into the "good and large land" prepared for my destiny.

El Roi, defend my family with Your watchful care. Break the grip of every oppressor, silence every tormenting voice, and overturn every plan of the enemy. Let Your seeing transform into saving, healing, and restoring power in every area of our lives.

I declare that I am not forsaken. I am not overlooked. The God who sees my affliction is the God who delivers me and ushers me into His promises. In Jesus' name, Amen.

65

Held as His Treasure

> "He found him in a desert land, in the waste howling wilderness. He surrounded him. He cared for him. He kept him as the apple of his eye. As an eagle that stirs up her nest, that flutters over her young, he spread abroad his wings, he took them, he bore them on his feathers."
> — Deuteronomy 32:10–11 WEB

Devotional Insight

El Roi sees you not as forgotten in the wilderness but as treasured, kept, and carried. This Scripture describes the profound tenderness of God's watchful care—finding you in barren places, surrounding you with His presence, and guarding you as the apple of His eye. The God who sees also shelters, instructs, and lifts you. Like an eagle stirring its young to grow yet hovering to protect, God guides you into maturity without abandoning you in the process. For the believer, this Name of God reveals a love that is protective, nurturing, and deeply invested. El Roi sees your vulnerability and responds with strength; He sees your needs and answers with covering; He sees your journey and supplies sustaining grace every step of the way.

Prayer

El Roi, my God who sees me and keeps me, I worship You for the tender strength of Your watchful care. You found me in seasons of emptiness, surrounded me when life felt harsh, and held me close as the apple of Your eye. Thank You for never abandoning me to the wilderness but carrying me through it.

Lord, surround me and my family with Your protective presence. Let Your wings overshadow our home. Let Your feathers carry us above every storm. When I feel weak, lift me. When I feel uncertain, guide me. When I feel threatened, shield me. You are the God who watches over me with unbroken attention and unchanging love.

Father, stir my heart toward growth, faith, and obedience, just as the eagle stirs its young. Do not let me settle in comfort zones that limit destiny. Teach me to rise, to trust, and to soar into the fullness of Your calling. Yet as You stretch me, hover over me. Let Your nearness be my safety and Your voice be my direction.

El Roi, let Your seeing become my confidence. You know every danger before it approaches, every need before it emerges, every fear before it forms. Keep me close. Keep me aligned. Keep me steady. Let my family be preserved under Your wings and carried by Your grace.

I declare that I am treasured, protected, and uplifted. The God who sees me is the God who carries me into promise and destiny. In Jesus' name, Amen.

66

Strengthened Under His Eyes

"For Yahweh's eyes run back and forth throughout the whole earth, to show himself strong in the behalf of those whose heart is perfect toward him. You have done foolishly in this; for from now on, you will have wars."
— 2 Chronicles 16:9 WEB

Devotional Insight

El Roi is not passive in His seeing; His eyes move with purpose, seeking those whose hearts lean toward Him so He may show Himself strong on their behalf. God watches over you not merely to observe but to intervene, strengthen, uphold, and reveal His might. This Scripture teaches that His seeing is connected to His support—where His eyes rest, His power flows. For the believer, this means that your sincerity, surrender, and trust draw divine strength into your circumstances. When your heart is toward Him, His strength is toward you. El Roi is actively scanning the earth to reinforce you in battles you cannot win alone, to fortify you where you feel weak, and to stand with you against every opposition. You are never unseen, never unsupported, and never without heavenly strength.

Prayer

El Roi, God whose eyes search the earth with holy intention, I thank You that Your gaze rests upon me. You do not simply watch—you strengthen. You do not merely see—you uphold. Today I yield my heart to You, knowing that as my heart aligns with Yours, Your power aligns with my needs.

Lord, show Yourself strong in my life. Let Your might break through every barrier hindering my progress. Let Your strength dismantle every enemy strategy. Let Your power fortify my spirit where weariness has crept in. I welcome Your intervention into every battle—spiritual, emotional, relational, financial, and generational.

El Roi, teach my heart to be steadfast before You. Strip away divided loyalties, doubtful thoughts, and hidden fears. Make my heart whole in its devotion so that nothing blocks the flow of Your strength. Fix my gaze where Yours rests—on truth, obedience, surrender, and faith.

Father, let Your eyes fall upon my family. Strengthen us where we are weak. Empower us where we feel overextended. Defend us where we are vulnerable. Let Your watchful care become a shield around our home, a fortress around our destiny, and a testimony to Your faithfulness.

I decree that I will not walk in my own strength but in the power of the God who sees me. I will not battle alone, for the eyes of El Roi are upon me, and His strength surrounds me. In Jesus' name, Amen.

67

Refined by His Seeing

"Behold, I go forward, but he is not there; and backward, but I can't perceive him. He works to the left hand, but I can't see him. He turns to the right hand, but I can't see him. But he knows the way that I take. When he has tried me, I will come out like gold."
— Job 23:8–10 WEB

Devotional Insight

There are seasons when God feels hidden, when you cannot sense His presence or see His hand. Yet El Roi reminds you that even when you cannot see Him, He sees you perfectly. Job couldn't locate God in any direction, but he rested in one unshakable truth: God knew his path. El Roi not only sees the road you walk but understands the refining purpose woven into every step. His seeing is reassuring—it means you are never lost, never aimless, and never abandoned in sorrow. The God who sees leads you through affliction and emerges you as gold. His gaze is the guiding force that ensures your pain becomes purpose, your testing produces purity, and your journey fulfills destiny.

Prayer

El Roi, my God who sees even when I cannot trace You, my heart leans into Your knowing today. There are moments when I do not feel You near, when the path ahead feels uncertain and the shadows feel overwhelming—but even then, You see me fully. Your watchful eye never loses sight of my steps.

Lord, You know the way that I take. You understand my journey more deeply than I do. When I feel blinded by circumstance, let Your seeing become my confidence. When I cannot discern Your nearness, let the truth of Your watchful presence anchor my soul. Refine me through every trial. Shape me through every challenge. Bring me out as gold—purified, strengthened, and deeply rooted in faith.

Father, guard my heart from discouragement when You seem silent. Remind me that silence is not absence and hiddenness is not abandonment. You are working even when unseen, orchestrating deliverance, preparing breakthroughs, and maturing my faith.

El Roi, look upon my family and refine what must be refined. Lead us through every season with Your unseen hand. Let the fire only remove what hinders destiny and let the outcome be glory, purity, and supernatural growth.

I declare that I am seen, known, and guided. Even when I cannot perceive God, He perceives me perfectly. My path is not dark to Him, and I will emerge victorious by His watchful care. In Jesus' name, Amen.

68

Held in His Compassion

> "You see it, for you see trouble and grief; you take it into your hand. You help the victim and the fatherless."
> — Psalm 10:14 WEB

Devotional Insight

El Roi is moved by what wounds you. He does not overlook sorrow, injustice, or hardship. Instead, He sees trouble and grief and takes them into His own hand. This reveals a God who is not emotionally distant but profoundly compassionate—a God who becomes the defender of the helpless and the helper of the afflicted. His seeing is active deliverance, not passive awareness. The believer can rest knowing that every burden, heartbreak, and injustice has already been noticed and taken up by the God who sees. You are not left to fend for yourself; El Roi rises on behalf of the weary and carries the pain that threatens to crush the soul. His seeing is your assurance that you are upheld, protected, and tenderly cared for.

Prayer

El Roi, You who see trouble and grief, I bring my heart before You knowing I am never unseen in my suffering. You take my pain into Your own hands. You respond with compassion, understanding, and power. Thank You for being the God who refuses to ignore affliction.

Lord, look upon every burden I carry today. See the griefs I do not speak aloud. See the pressures weighing upon my soul. See the unseen battles in my heart. Take each one into Your hand and minister healing, strength, and victory. Let Your compassion saturate every wounded place within me.

Father, rise as my Helper. Where injustice has attacked me, defend me. Where sorrow has drained me, restore me. Where fear has tried to silence me, empower me. Let the comfort of Your seeing settle deeply into my spirit, reminding me that I am never alone or abandoned.

El Roi, extend Your compassion to my family. See every need, every struggle, every silent cry. Lift us into Your peace. Shield us from harm. Heal what is broken. Provide what is lacking. And draw each of us closer to Your heart of love.

I declare that my trouble is not ignored, my grief is not wasted, and my future is not threatened. The God who sees takes my burden into His hand, and His help transforms my life. In Jesus' name, Amen.

69

Kept Under His Eye

> "I have called on you, for you will answer me, God. Turn your ear to me. Hear my speech. Show your marvelous loving kindness, you who save those who take refuge by your right hand from their enemies. Keep me as the apple of your eye. Hide me under the shadow of your wings…"
> — Psalm 17:6–8 WEB

Devotional Insight

El Roi not only sees you—He treasures you. To be the "apple of His eye" is to be the point of His most tender and protective gaze. This Scripture reveals that the God who sees responds with love, answers prayer, shields from enemies, and covers you with His wings. His sight becomes your safety, His nearness your refuge, and His kindness your anchor. For the believer, El Roi is the One who hears every call, cares deeply about every concern, and protects with unstoppable devotion. You are not exposed to danger; you are hidden beneath divine wings, continually kept in God's line of love.

Prayer

El Roi, Keeper of my life, I call upon You knowing You hear, You answer, and You protect. You do not simply see me—you delight in me. You set Your gaze upon me as the apple of Your eye, and under that gaze, I find safety beyond human comprehension.

Lord, let Your marvelous lovingkindness surround me. Hide me beneath the shadow of Your wings. Let every attack of the enemy fall powerless because I am covered. Let every whisper of fear be silenced because I am kept. Let every storm lose its force because I dwell beneath Your protection.

Father, keep me in Your sight. Guard my heart from harm, my steps from danger, and my mind from torment. Let Your watchful care create a barrier that no weapon can penetrate. I rest in the assurance that nothing touches my life without passing through Your love.

El Roi, extend Your protective wings over my family. Keep us as the apple of Your eye. Shield our comings and goings, defend our health, bless our endeavors, and guide our decisions. Let Your presence be a fortress around our home.

I declare that I am hidden, treasured, and protected. The God who sees me keeps me under His wings, and no enemy can prevail against His covering. In Jesus' name, Amen.

70

Rejoicing in His Seeing

> "I will be glad and rejoice in your loving kindness, for you have seen my affliction. You have known my soul in adversities."
> — Psalm 31:7 WEB

Devotional Insight

El Roi brings joy because His seeing is evidence of His love. God does not simply notice affliction—He enters into it with understanding and compassion. He knows your soul in adversity, which means your internal battles are as visible to Him as outward circumstances. For the believer, this is a source of deep comfort: nothing about your struggle is invisible to God. His lovingkindness surrounds you because He has seen every hardship and fully comprehends every layer of your pain. The God who sees is the God who stays, supports, and saves.

Prayer

El Roi, the God who sees my affliction, I rejoice in Your lovingkindness. Your vision of my life is not distant—it is intimate, compassionate, and filled with mercy. You know my soul in adversity. You understand what I carry even when I cannot express it. Thank You for being so near, so attentive, and so faithful.

Lord, let Your lovingkindness be the atmosphere of my heart today. Where affliction has pressed against me, let Your comfort press back. Where adversity has shaken me, let Your presence stabilize me. Where sorrow has lingered, let Your joy rise like morning light.

Father, look upon every difficult area of my life. See every hidden struggle—spiritual battles, emotional wounds, relational tensions, financial stress, and inner fears. Let Your seeing bring healing, clarity, and divine intervention. Lift me above adversity and establish me in peace.

El Roi, look with compassion upon my family. Know our souls. Understand our adversities. Bring relief where there has been pressure, restoration where there has been loss, and victory where there has been warfare. Let Your lovingkindness rewrite every painful chapter with hope.

I declare that because God sees me, I am strengthened. Because He knows me, I am sustained. Because His lovingkindness surrounds me, I will rejoice even in adversity. In Jesus' name, Amen.

71

Guided by His Instruction

"I will instruct you and teach you in the way which you shall go. I will counsel you with my eye on you."

— Psalm 32:8 WEB

Devotional Insight

El Roi is not only the God who sees—you are guided by His seeing. His eye does more than observe; it directs, counsels, and leads with wisdom that flows from perfect knowledge. This Scripture reveals the intimacy of His guidance: He instructs you personally, teaches you lovingly, and counsels you attentively. For the believer, this means you are never left to navigate life blindly. God's watchful eye ensures you are kept from wrong paths and led into right ones. His seeing provides clarity where confusion exists, assurance where fear tries to speak, and direction where uncertainty lingers. El Roi guides with care, compassion, and precision.

Prayer

El Roi, You who guide me with Your loving gaze, I surrender my path to You today. Thank You that Your eye is upon me—not to judge me but to counsel, instruct, and shepherd me. I receive Your promise to teach me the way I should go.

Lord, illuminate the steps before me. Where decisions feel heavy, speak wisdom. Where confusion tries to cloud my heart, release Your clarity. Lead me in paths of righteousness, peace, and divine purpose. Let Your eye be my compass, Your counsel my direction, and Your presence my safety.

Father, guard me from detours and distractions. Reveal the traps of the enemy before I step into them. Show me the difference between good opportunities and God-appointed ones. Shape my discernment so I can recognize Your leading even in subtle whispers.

El Roi, let Your eye be upon my family. Teach us, guide us, and direct our steps. Order our priorities, align our hearts with Your will, and protect us from wrong connections, wrong decisions, and wrong paths. Let our household walk under Your instruction and flourish under Your counsel.

I declare that I do not walk in darkness or confusion. The God who sees me guides me. His eye is upon me, instructing my steps and securing my destiny. In Jesus' name, Amen.

72

Observed by Heaven

"Yahweh looks from heaven. He sees all the sons of men. From the place of his habitation he looks out on all the inhabitants of the earth, he who fashions all of their hearts; and he considers all of their works."
— Psalm 33:13–15 WEB

Devotional Insight

El Roi is the God who sees from heaven with perfect clarity, understanding every heart and every action. His seeing is not distant observation—it is intentional oversight rooted in His role as Creator. He fashioned your heart, so He understands its motives, desires, and struggles. He considers your works, meaning He evaluates your life with wisdom, compassion, and truth. This Scripture reminds the believer that God's heavenly perspective is not detached but deeply engaged. He watches over you with full knowledge of what you face, what you need, and what He has designed you to become. His seeing provides reassurance that nothing about your life is random or unnoticed.

Prayer

El Roi, You who look from heaven and see every detail of my life, I honor You today. Your gaze is not distant—it is full of understanding, compassion, and sovereign purpose. Thank You for fashioning my heart and knowing me more deeply than I know myself.

Lord, since You see all, I invite Your wisdom into my decisions and Your clarity into my thoughts. Consider my works and refine them. Purify my motives, align my desires, and strengthen my actions so they reflect Your heart. Let nothing in me resist Your shaping hand.

Father, watch over my life from heaven's vantage point. See the places where I need Your intervention. See the battles I cannot fight alone. See the burdens that weigh upon me. From Your throne, send help, counsel, and breakthrough. Let heaven respond to what You see in my life.

El Roi, look upon my family with the same tender attention. You have fashioned all our hearts. Consider our works. Guide us into righteousness, unity, and purpose. Let Your heavenly oversight protect us, prosper us, and prepare us for the plans You established before time began.

I declare that I live under divine observation—not for judgment, but for guidance and protection. The God who sees from heaven directs my steps on earth. In Jesus' name, Amen.

73

Rescued in His Nearness

> "Yahweh's eyes are toward the righteous. His ears listen to their cry. Yahweh's face is against those who do evil, to cut off their memory from the earth. The righteous cry, and Yahweh hears, and delivers them out of all their troubles. Yahweh is near to those who have a broken heart, and saves those who have a crushed spirit."
> — Psalm 34:15–18 WEB

Devotional Insight

El Roi's seeing draws Him near. His eyes are fixed on the righteous—those who fear Him, trust Him, and walk with Him. He listens to their cries, hears their pleas, and rescues them from trouble. His seeing is paired with nearness, compassion, and deliverance. For the believer, this means that in moments of heartbreak or spiritual crushing, God does not distance Himself—He comes closer. He watches over you with love, responds to your cry, and moves to save. El Roi is attentive to your pain and active in your deliverance.

Prayer

El Roi, whose eyes are upon the righteous and whose ears listen to their cry, I come before You with gratitude and reverence. Thank You for watching over me with compassion, for hearing every whisper of my heart, and for promising deliverance in times of trouble.

Lord, turn Your face toward my cry today. Look upon my pain, my pressures, and my silent tears. Let Your nearness comfort my broken heart. Let Your saving power lift my crushed spirit. Where I feel weary, strengthen me. Where I feel wounded, heal me. Where I feel overwhelmed, rescue me.

Father, deliver me from every trouble—seen and unseen. Break the assignments of the enemy. Cancel the plans of darkness. Uproot every form of evil seeking to operate around me. Let Your presence surround me as a shield, and let Your eyes guard my path with holy vigilance.

El Roi, be near to my family. See our struggles. Hear our cries. Save us from every affliction. Bind up the brokenhearted among us and strengthen the crushed. Let Your deliverance sweep through our household, establishing peace, restoration, and divine order.

I declare that I am not alone, not abandoned, not unheard. The God who sees me is near to me, hears my cry, and delivers me from all my troubles. In Jesus' name, Amen.

74

My Tears in His Book

"You count my wanderings. You put my tears into your bottle. Aren't they in your book? Then my enemies shall turn back in the day that I call. I know this, that God is for me."
— Psalm 56:8–9 WEB

Devotional Insight

El Roi is the God who records every detail of your journey—your wanderings, your tears, your battles, and your victories. Nothing slips past His attention. Your tears are not wasted; they are treasured. Your wanderings are not meaningless; they are counted. Your cries are not ignored; they move heaven. This Scripture reveals the depth of God's personal care: He preserves your tears as testimonies, and He stores your journey in His book. For the believer, this means God is fully invested in your story. El Roi sees what hurts you, remembers what you've endured, and rises in your defense when you call upon Him.

Prayer

El Roi, You who count my wanderings and collect my tears, I worship You for Your intimate care. Nothing in my life is hidden from Your gaze. You see the moments I break, the nights I cry, and the days I feel lost—and You treasure what others overlook.

Lord, take every tear I've shed and turn them into seeds of future joy. Let the pain I've endured produce glory. Let the wanderings I've walked become pathways into purpose. When I call upon You, let every enemy retreat. Let every adversarial force lose power. Let every attack be reversed because the God who sees me stands with me.

Father, remind my heart daily that You are for me. Silence every lie that tells me otherwise. Let the record You keep of my journey become evidence of Your faithfulness, protection, and covenant love.

El Roi, look upon my family and gather our tears. Heal our wounds, comfort our hearts, and strengthen our journeys. Let not a single moment of our pain be wasted. Turn every sorrow into testimony and every wandering into wisdom.

I declare that God is for me. My enemies turn back. My story is known by heaven. My tears are remembered by God. The God who sees me defends me with unstoppable love. In Jesus' name, Amen.

75

Surrounded by His Knowing

"Yahweh, you have searched me, and you know me. You know my sitting down and my rising up. You perceive my thoughts from afar. You search out my path and my lying down, and are acquainted with all my ways. For there is not a word on my tongue, but, behold, Yahweh, you know it altogether. You hem me in behind and before. You laid your hand on me. This knowledge is beyond me. It's lofty. I can't attain it. Where could I go from your Spirit? Or where could I flee from your presence? If I ascend up into heaven, you are there. If I make my bed in Sheol, behold, you are there! If I take the wings of the dawn, and settle in the uttermost parts of the sea, even there your hand will lead me, and your right hand will hold me. If I say, 'Surely the darkness will overwhelm me. The light around me will be night,' even the darkness doesn't hide from you, but the night shines as the day. The darkness is like light to you."
— Psalm 139:1–12 WEB

Devotional Insight

El Roi knows you fully, sees you completely, and surrounds you continuously. This Scripture reveals the depth of His involvement in your life—your movements, thoughts, words, habits, fears, and destinations are all within His gaze. His seeing is not surveillance; it is shepherding. It is the care of a God who refuses to let darkness overwhelm you or distance separate you from His presence. No place is too far, no moment too hidden, and no emotion too deep for His eyes to reach you. For the believer, this brings tremendous peace: you are never lost, never unnoticed, and never beyond the reach of God's leading hand.

Prayer

El Roi, You who search me and know me, I stand in holy awe of Your intimate knowledge of my life. You see every detail—my rhythms, my thoughts, my words, my weaknesses, and my ways. Yet Your seeing is filled with love, not condemnation. Thank You for surrounding me behind and before, and for laying Your hand upon me.

Lord, lead me with Your hand wherever I go. Whether I ascend into joy or descend into difficulty, let Your presence guide me. When I feel overwhelmed, remind me that darkness is never dark to You. When I feel lost, remind me that Your eyes pierce every shadow. When I feel distant, remind me that Your Spirit is already there.

Father, I give You access to every hidden part of my heart. Search me. Cleanse me. Strengthen me. Redirect me.

Where sin tries to hide, expose it. Where fear tries to grip, break it. Where confusion tries to cloud, lift it. Let the God who sees be the God who heals and transforms.

El Roi, look upon my family and surround us with Your presence. Hem us in behind and before. Lead us in truth. Hold us in Your right hand. Let no darkness overshadow our home and no trial separate us from Your guidance.

I declare that I am fully seen, fully known, and fully kept by God. There is no place I walk where His eyes do not follow and His presence does not accompany. In Jesus' name, Amen.

76

Seen in Every Path

"For the ways of man are before Yahweh's eyes.
He examines all his paths."
— Proverbs 5:21 WEB

Devotional Insight

El Roi sees every path you walk—every choice, every turn, every hidden motive, every quiet struggle. Nothing about your journey is obscure or unnoticed to Him. His seeing is not meant to condemn but to protect and guide. When Scripture says He examines all your paths, it reveals His desire to keep you from danger, to redirect you when you drift, and to preserve your life from the traps of the enemy and the snares of self-deception. For the believer, this means there is no confusion so thick, no temptation so subtle, and no circumstance so complex that God's eyes cannot pierce through it. El Roi watches your steps with wisdom, tenderness, and unwavering commitment to your destiny.

Prayer

El Roi, You who examine all my paths, I surrender my journey into Your watchful care. You see the roads I choose, the ones I avoid, the ones I stumble through, and the ones I do not yet understand. Thank You for keeping my ways before Your eyes, for refusing to let me walk alone or unprotected.

Lord, shine Your light upon every path I am walking. Where I am misaligned, realign me. Where danger is ahead, warn me. Where deception lurks, expose it. Let Your seeing deliver me from choices that would lead to regret or destruction. Guard my steps with Your wisdom and steady my heart with Your truth.

Father, examine my motives and purify my intentions. Remove hidden pride, impatience, fear, or compromise. Shape my path into one that reflects Your righteousness, peace, and purpose. Let every decision I make be influenced by Your counsel and overseen by Your loving gaze.

El Roi, look upon my family and examine our paths as well. Keep us from wrong associations, harmful influences, and destructive patterns. Guide us into Your will with clarity and strength. Let our home walk securely because Your eyes are upon us.

I declare that my steps are not blind, my decisions are not unguided, and my future is not uncertain. The God who sees all my paths is directing my way into safety, blessing, and destiny. In Jesus' name, Amen.

77

Upheld by His Righteous Right Hand

"You whom I have taken hold of from the ends of the earth, and called from its corners, and said to you, 'You are my servant, I have chosen you and not cast you away.' Don't you be afraid, for I am with you. Don't be dismayed, for I am your God. I will strengthen you. Yes, I will help you. I will uphold you with the right hand of my righteousness."
— Isaiah 41:9–10 WEB

Devotional Insight

El Roi sees you as chosen and held—not abandoned. This Scripture reveals a God who not only sees but intervenes, selects, calls, strengthens, and upholds. His eyes ensure you are never lost in the world's chaos or forgotten in life's trials. Because He sees you, He secures you. Because He sees you, He strengthens you. Because He sees you, He stays with you. For the believer, this passage is a reminder that fear has no place when the God who sees is also the God who supports. His righteous right hand is the unshakable foundation beneath your life.

Prayer

El Roi, my God who has chosen me and refuses to cast me away, I worship You for Your steadfast care. You saw me at the ends of the earth, in vulnerable places, in forgotten seasons, and You called me by name. I thank You that Your seeing led to my choosing, and Your choosing led to my keeping.

Lord, uproot every fear within me. Let the truth of Your presence silence anxiety. Let the assurance that You are my God break the power of discouragement. Strengthen me in every area where I feel weak. Help me where I feel overwhelmed. Uphold me where I feel like collapsing under pressure.

Father, let Your righteous right hand lift me above every attack, every lie, every heavy burden, and every spiritual assault. Sustain me when I am weary. Empower me when I feel inadequate. Cover me with Your strength until opposition loses its grip and weariness breaks.

El Roi, look upon my family and let this same promise stand. Uphold us together. Strengthen us individually. Help us corporately. Let no member of my household fall into fear, discouragement, or despair. Your seeing is our stability, Your presence our peace, and Your hand our protection.

I declare that I am strengthened, supported, and secured. The God who sees me is the God who upholds me with His righteous right hand. In Jesus' name, Amen.

78

Protected in the Waters and Fire

"But now Yahweh who created you, Jacob, and he who formed you, Israel, says: 'Don't be afraid, for I have redeemed you. I have called you by your name. You are mine. When you pass through the waters, I will be with you; and through the rivers, they will not overflow you. When you walk through the fire, you will not be burned, and flame will not scorch you.'"
— Isaiah 43:1-2 WEB

Devotional Insight

El Roi sees every trial you face—deep waters, overwhelming rivers, and fiery trials. But He does more than observe; He walks with you through them. This Scripture reveals that you are not unseen in adversity. You are redeemed, named, and claimed by God Himself. His seeing ensures His presence, and His presence ensures your preservation. For the believer, this means no trial consumes you, no river overtakes you, and no fire destroys you. The God who sees you is the God who stands with you.

Prayer

El Roi, You who call me by name and declare, "You are mine," I rest in the strength of Your love. You see my trials, my pressures, my waters, and my fires—not from a distance but from beside me. Thank You for being the God who walks with me through every storm.

Lord, when the waters rise, be my stability. When the rivers rage, be my anchor. When the fire intensifies, be my protection. Let none of these overwhelm me because Your presence surrounds me. Let every intimidating circumstance lose its power in the light of Your promise.

Father, speak redemption over every area of my life where shame or struggle has lingered. Remind me that I am Yours—chosen, claimed, and kept. Let this identity silence every fear, every lie, and every doubt. Hold me steady through adversity until I emerge refined, preserved, and victorious.

El Roi, look upon my family and walk with us through every hardship. Let no danger consume us, no flood swallow us, no fire scorch us. Surround our home with Your mighty presence. Shield our minds, guard our hearts, and preserve our peace.

I declare that I do not walk alone. The God who sees me walks with me. Waters cannot drown me. Flames cannot consume me. I am redeemed, named, and kept. In Jesus' name, Amen.

79

Engraved on His Hands

> "Can a woman forget her nursing child, that she should not have compassion on the son of her womb? Yes, these may forget, yet I will not forget you! Behold, I have engraved you on the palms of my hands. Your walls are continually before me."
> — Isaiah 49:15–16 WEB

Devotional Insight

El Roi's seeing is anchored in covenantal memory. God does not merely watch you—He remembers you with eternal commitment. Even if the deepest human bond could fail, God declares that His compassion cannot. You are engraved on His palms—permanently, personally, and lovingly. Your walls—your needs, battles, limitations, and vulnerabilities—are continually before Him. For the believer, this means you are never forgotten and never out of sight. God's remembrance guarantees His care, protection, and provision.

Prayer

El Roi, the God who never forgets me, I bow in gratitude and awe. Thank You that I am engraved on the palms of Your hands. Thank You that Your compassion toward me surpasses even the strongest natural love. Thank You that my life, my walls, my needs, and my battles are continually before You.

Lord, let this truth heal every wound of rejection and silence every feeling of abandonment. Let me never again doubt Your nearness or Your care. Your eyes are upon me continually, and Your hands carry the record of my life. I am not forgotten—I am held.

Father, build up every broken wall in my life. Strengthen my boundaries, restore my defenses, and repair what the enemy has attempted to breach. Let Your remembrance turn into intervention. Let Your compassion turn into provision. Let Your seeing turn into deliverance.

El Roi, look upon my family with this same unfailing compassion. Keep us engraved in Your hands. Remember our prayers, defend our destiny, and surround our home with heavenly attention and divine care.

I declare that I am remembered, beloved, and engraved upon His hands. The God who sees me cannot forget me, and His compassion upholds my life. In Jesus' name, Amen.

80

Known Before I Began

"Before I formed you in the womb, I knew you. Before you were born, I sanctified you. I have appointed you a prophet to the nations. Then I said, 'Ah, Lord Yahweh! Behold, I don't know how to speak; for I am a child.' But Yahweh said to me, 'Don't say, "I am a child;" for you must go to whomever I send you, and whatever I command you, you must speak. Don't be afraid because of them, for I am with you to rescue you,' says Yahweh."
— Jeremiah 1:5–8 WEB

Devotional Insight

El Roi saw you before anyone else did. His knowledge of you predates your birth, your calling, your insecurities, and your experiences. He formed you with intention, sanctified you with purpose, and appointed you before life ever introduced challenges. Because He sees your destiny, He refuses to let your fears define you. El Roi not only sees who you are but who you will become. For the believer, this reveals a God who equips, directs, and protects you as you walk in your calling.

Prayer

El Roi, You who knew me before I existed, I worship You for the intentionality of Your creation. You saw my destiny before I took my first breath. You formed me with purpose, sanctified me with calling, and appointed me with divine intention. Thank You for seeing greatness in me even when I struggle to see it myself.

Lord, break every limitation I have spoken over my life. Silence every insecurity that says, "I am too young, too weak, too unqualified, or too afraid." Let Your words—"You must go… you must speak… I am with you"—echo louder than my fears. Strengthen me to walk boldly in what You have ordained.

Father, rescue me from every fear of people, every voice of intimidation, and every force that seeks to hinder my assignment. Let Your presence empower my obedience. Let Your seeing affirm my identity. Let Your calling propel my actions.

El Roi, look upon my family and reveal that same pre-designed purpose over each one. Remind us that we were formed intentionally, known intimately, and appointed divinely. Let destiny awaken, confidence arise, and obedience flourish.

I declare that I am known, called, equipped, and protected. The God who saw me before my beginning is with me through every step of my destiny. In Jesus' name, Amen.

81

Watched with Intentional Goodness

"You, Yahweh, know me. You see me, and test my heart toward you. Pull them out like sheep for the slaughter, and prepare them for the day of slaughter."
— Jeremiah 12:3 WEB

Devotional Insight

El Roi is the God who knows you intimately and sees you with perfect understanding. His testing is not to destroy but to reveal purity, strengthen character, and align your heart with His will. Jeremiah knew that God's sight was both discerning and protective—that He sees not only the heart of the righteous but also the schemes of the wicked. For the believer, this Scripture reveals a God who does not allow hidden evil to triumph, nor does He permit the righteous to remain vulnerable. His seeing becomes your shield, His knowledge becomes your safety, and His justice becomes your vindication. El Roi watches your life with intention, ensuring that evil is exposed and goodness prevails.

Prayer

El Roi, You who know me fully and see every detail of my heart, I bow before You in trust and surrender. Your eyes search me with truth and love, refining what must be refined and strengthening what must be strengthened. Thank You for seeing my motives, my intentions, and my longing to walk uprightly before You.

Lord, where my heart needs testing, test me. Where impurities linger, purify me. Where fear or doubt tries to settle, uproot them. Let Your gaze cleanse me and shape me into a vessel worthy of Your calling. Teach me to desire what You desire, to love what You love, and to walk boldly in righteousness.

Father, You also see the workings of the wicked—every plot, every deceit, every invisible attack. Let Your justice rise. Expose schemes designed to harm me or my family. Pull out the works of darkness and dismantle every device of the enemy. Let no hidden evil find success around my life.

El Roi, keep Your eyes upon my family. Test our hearts, strengthen our spirits, and guard our paths. Let Your justice defend us, Your mercy surround us, and Your righteousness establish us. May Your seeing secure our destiny and silence every adversarial force.

I declare that I am known, examined, and defended by the God who sees me. His justice prevails, His protection surrounds me, and His purpose stands firm in my life. In Jesus' name, Amen.

82

Planted Under His Watchful Care

"For I will set my eyes on them for good, and I will bring them again to this land. I will build them, and not pull them down; and I will plant them, and not pluck them up."
— Jeremiah 24:6 WEB

Devotional Insight

El Roi sets His eyes on you *for good*. His seeing brings restoration, stability, and divine rebuilding. In this Scripture, God promises not only to return His people to their rightful place but also to build and plant them in ways that no enemy can uproot. For the believer, this reveals that God's gaze carries intention—He watches over you with the purpose of securing your destiny, establishing your future, and protecting your growth. Where destruction once lived, He builds. Where instability once reigned, He plants. Where fear once dominated, He restores. El Roi's eyes are upon you for blessing, not harm.

Prayer

El Roi, God whose eyes are set upon me for good, I rejoice in Your loving oversight. Your gaze brings hope to barren places, rebuilding to broken foundations, and planting to uprooted areas. Thank You for watching over me not with judgment but with redemptive intention.

Lord, rebuild what has been torn down in my life. Restore what the enemy has tried to break. Strengthen what has grown weak. Plant me in purpose, in stability, and in the soil of Your will. Let my roots go deep into Your faithfulness and let my fruit glorify Your name.

Father, bring me again into every promise You have spoken. Return me to territories of calling and influence. Position me in the land You destined for me before time began. Let nothing uproot what You plant, and let no force tear down what You build.

El Roi, watch over my family with this same goodness. Build us where we need strength. Plant us where we need stability. Restore what needs healing. Let Your eyes secure our inheritance and Your hand preserve our future.

I declare that I am upheld by the God whose eyes are set on me for good. He builds, He plants, and He establishes my destiny in strength. In Jesus' name, Amen.

83

Seen, Heard, and Strengthened

"Then he said to me, 'Don't be afraid, Daniel; for from the first day that you set your heart to understand, and to humble yourself before your God, your words were heard:' for I have come for your words."
— Daniel 10:12 WEB

Devotional Insight

El Roi sees the posture of your heart before He hears the words of your mouth. Daniel's humility and desire for understanding triggered heaven's response long before breakthrough manifested. God saw his intention, heard his prayer from day one, and dispatched angelic assistance on his behalf. For the believer, this reveals that God's seeing is immediate, His hearing is attentive, and His response is active—even when delays appear. El Roi sees your heart's cry, your humility, and your longing for His will, and He moves in ways you cannot see yet. Your prayers are never lost; they activate heaven's intervention.

Prayer

El Roi, God who sees my heart before my words, I thank You for Your immediate attention to my prayers. You notice the posture of humility, the longing for understanding, and the sincerity of my pursuit. Thank You that from the first day I seek You, You respond.

Lord, strengthen me in seasons where answers seem delayed. Remind me that heaven has already moved on my behalf. Let my heart remain steadfast, humble, and aligned with Your will. Remove every fear that whispers that You have not heard or do not care. Let Your peace settle over my spirit as I trust in Your unseen activity.

Father, release angelic assistance into every area of my life where battles rage behind the scenes. Let every hindrance be removed, every delay be broken, and every spiritual resistance be shattered. Arise and bring forth the manifestation of what You already initiated.

El Roi, look upon my family and respond to our prayers with the same swiftness. See our humility, hear our cries, and release Your power. Let our words—prayers, decrees, intercessions—draw heavenly intervention and divine strength.

I declare that my prayers are heard, my heart is seen, and my breakthrough is in motion. The God who sees me has already sent help. In Jesus' name, Amen.

84

Rewarded in the Secret Place

"...that your charitable deed may be in secret, and your Father who sees in secret will reward you openly."
— Matthew 6:4 WEB

Devotional Insight

El Roi sees what others overlook—your quiet obedience, hidden sacrifices, private generosity, and unseen faithfulness. This Scripture reveals that God values what is done in secret with pure motives. His seeing is not for shame but for reward. He notices every act of righteousness you perform without applause. He takes note of every sacrifice you make out of love for Him. For the believer, this means that nothing done for God is wasted. The God who sees in secret honors openly, ensuring that your reward comes from Him and not from people.

Prayer

El Roi, the God who sees in secret, I honor You for valuing what others never notice. Thank You for watching the quiet places of my heart, my obedience, my generosity, and my devotion. I choose to serve You without seeking human recognition, knowing that Your reward is greater than anything man can give.

Lord, purify my motives. Let everything I do—giving, serving, praying, helping—flow from love and reverence for You. Keep my heart free from pride, performance, or the desire for approval. Let me find joy in pleasing You alone.

Father, see my secret sacrifices and breathe upon them. See the prayers I prayed in silence, the tears I shed in private, the offerings I gave without announcement. Let every seed sown in hidden obedience produce a harvest of open blessing, breakthrough, and favor according to Your Word.

El Roi, extend this blessing to my family. See the unseen labors, efforts, sacrifices, and commitments made behind the scenes. Let open reward, divine favor, and supernatural increase manifest in every area of our life because You saw our hearts.

I declare that I work for the eyes of God and not the applause of man. The God who sees in secret will reward me openly. In Jesus' name, Amen.

85

Numbered and Protected

> "Aren't two sparrows sold for an assarion? Not one of them falls on the ground apart from your Father's will, but the very hairs of your head are all numbered. Therefore don't be afraid. You are of more value than many sparrows."
> — Matthew 10:29–31 WEB

Devotional Insight

El Roi's seeing is so detailed, so intimate, and so attentive that even the hairs of your head are numbered. Nothing in your life is overlooked—not your value, not your vulnerability, and certainly not your destiny. If God watches over sparrows, He watches over you with infinitely greater care. For the believer, this Scripture destroys fear and insecurity. Your worth is established by the God who sees you continually. His attention to your life proves His commitment to your protection and provision. You are never forgotten, never insignificant, and never unprotected.

Prayer

El Roi, God who numbers the hairs on my head, I rest in the assurance of Your astonishing care. Your attention to my life is detailed beyond comprehension. You notice every change, every need, every fear, and every threat. Thank You that nothing touches me without first passing under Your watchful eye.

Lord, break the power of fear in my life. Let the revelation of Your valuing love shatter anxiety, insecurity, and worry. Remind me daily that I matter to You—not casually, but completely. If You watch the sparrow, You surely watch me.

Father, protect me from harm—physical, spiritual, emotional, and financial. Surround my steps with divine preservation. Let every plot of the enemy fail before it forms. Let every danger be diverted before it approaches. Let every need be met before it becomes a crisis. Your seeing is my safety.

El Roi, watch over my family with this same tender care. Number our hairs, guard our lives, and preserve our future. Let fear be far from our home and confidence rise within us because we are so deeply valued by You.

I declare that I am precious in the sight of God. I am watched, valued, and protected. The God who sees me will never abandon me. In Jesus' name, Amen.

86

Moved with Compassion Toward Me

"When the Lord saw her, he had compassion on her, and said to her, 'Don't cry.'"
— Luke 7:13 WEB

Devotional Insight

El Roi is not only the God who sees—He is the God who is moved. When Jesus saw the grieving widow, His seeing immediately activated compassion. He didn't wait for her to pray, plead, or explain; He saw her pain and responded. This reveals the tender heart of God toward every believer who carries sorrow, disappointment, or loss. His seeing is not distant observation—it is intimate involvement. El Roi looks upon your pain with mercy and steps toward you with healing. He meets you at the point of your tears and speaks life, comfort, and restoration. You are never unseen in your grief; you are deeply held in His compassion.

Prayer

El Roi, God who sees me and is moved with compassion, I come before You with every burden of my heart. Thank You for being the God who notices my tears and does not ignore my pain. You lean into my sorrow, and You comfort me with Your presence.

Lord, speak over me the same words You spoke to the grieving widow: "Don't cry." Let Your voice calm the storms within me. Let Your compassion wipe away the heaviness in my soul. Let Your nearness become my healing. Where grief has lingered, bring comfort. Where disappointment has settled, bring hope. Where fear has grown, bring peace.

Father, look upon my family with the same compassionate gaze. See every place where sadness, worry, or loss has tried to take root. Step into our lives and breathe new strength, new joy, new restoration. Let Your touch reverse what sorrow has damaged and revive what pain has suppressed.

El Roi, thank You for not requiring perfect prayers to respond. You see my heart even when my words fail. You see my tears even when I try to hide them. You see my longings even before I speak them. Let Your compassion manifest in breakthroughs, healing, and divine intervention.

I declare that I am seen, comforted, and restored by the God whose compassion moves Him toward me. My tears are not wasted, and my sorrow will not have the final word. In Jesus' name, Amen.

87

Known by the Good Shepherd

"I am the good shepherd. I know my own, and I'm known by my own."
— John 10:14 WEB

Devotional Insight

El Roi is revealed in Jesus, the Good Shepherd who knows His sheep intimately. To be "known" by God means you are understood, pursued, protected, and valued. The Shepherd does not lose sight of His flock—not in danger, not in darkness, not in confusion. His seeing is relational, not mechanical. He watches over you with affection and leads you with wisdom. For the believer, this Scripture reveals a God who doesn't just see your movements but understands your heart. You are neither anonymous nor forgotten; you are personally and deeply known by the One who guides your steps.

Prayer

El Roi, my Good Shepherd, I bless You for knowing me fully and calling me Your own. You see every detail of my life—my struggles, my desires, my weaknesses, my strengths—and yet You love me completely. Thank You for shepherding me with such tender faithfulness.

Lord, lead me with Your voice. Guide me into safe pastures and away from harmful paths. Let me recognize Your whispers, follow Your direction, and rest in Your presence. Keep me close to Your side, where fear cannot survive and confusion cannot mislead.

Father, protect me from wolves—visible and invisible. Guard my mind from lies, my heart from deception, and my steps from danger. Let Your rod and staff comfort, correct, and preserve me. I trust Your leadership because You know me better than I know myself.

El Roi, look upon my family and shepherd each one. Guard us from straying, guide us into purpose, and watch over our spiritual growth. Let Your knowledge of us shape our identity and ground our confidence. Surround our home with Your protective presence.

I declare that I am known, led, and kept by the Good Shepherd. His eyes are upon me, His voice guides me, and His love sustains me. In Jesus' name, Amen.

88

Laid Bare Before His Eyes

> "There is no creature that is hidden from his sight; but all things are naked and laid open before the eyes of him with whom we have to do."
> — Hebrews 4:13 WEB

Devotional Insight

El Roi sees everything—nothing is hidden, concealed, or overlooked. His sight penetrates beyond appearance into motives, thoughts, and depths of the soul. Although this truth is humbling, it is also profoundly freeing. Because God sees everything, you don't have to pretend, hide, or fear being misunderstood. His seeing brings accountability, healing, and alignment with His will. For the believer, this Scripture is a reminder that transparency before God leads to transformation. El Roi sees you completely, yet loves you wholly, and invites you into a life of honesty and holiness under His watchful care.

Prayer

El Roi, God before whom nothing is hidden, I stand before You with humility and openness. Thank You for seeing every part of my life—not to shame me, but to heal me. You see my strengths and my struggles, my obedience and my weakness, my faith and my flaws. I trust Your sight because it is full of mercy and truth.

Lord, search me and cleanse me. Remove every hidden sin, silent fear, and buried wound. Let nothing in me resist Your refining gaze. Shine Your light into the deepest places of my heart and bring transformation where I need it most.

Father, let Your seeing produce freedom. Strip away masks, excuses, and self-deception. Teach me to walk in truth, purity, and transparency. Align my inner life with Your Word so that my outer life reflects Your glory. Where shame tries to hide me, let Your grace bring me into the open.

El Roi, look upon my family and purify us. Remove hidden battles we have not acknowledged, heal wounds we have not spoken, and bring light to areas that need restoration. Let the God who sees bring deliverance into every corner of our home.

I declare that nothing in me is hidden from God, and nothing in me is beyond His healing. The God who sees all is the God who restores all. In Jesus' name, Amen.

89

Beholding His Eyes Upon Me

"For the eyes of the Lord are on the righteous, and his ears open to their prayer; but the face of the Lord is against those who do evil."
— 1 Peter 3:12 WEB

Devotional Insight

El Roi continually watches over the righteous. His eyes are not fleeting glances—they are fixed with intention, love, and protection. He listens to your prayers with eagerness and responds with Fatherly care. At the same time, His face is set against evil, ensuring that wicked plans do not prevail. For the believer, this Scripture offers bold assurance: Your prayers reach a God whose eyes are on you and whose ears are open. You are under divine surveillance for your good, and God's justice actively works on your behalf.

Prayer

El Roi, God whose eyes are upon me, I thank You for Your unwavering attention and Your listening ear. Your watchfulness brings comfort, and Your attentiveness brings confidence. Thank You for hearing my prayers—not occasionally, but continually.

Lord, let Your eyes guard my path. Watch over every decision, every step, and every moment of my life. Let Your favor surround me, Your wisdom guide me, and Your protection shield me. Keep me aligned with righteousness so that nothing hinders my prayers or obstructs Your blessings.

Father, turn Your face against every evil that seeks to harm me or my family. Frustrate the plans of darkness, disarm every weapon, and dismantle every scheme. Let Your justice prevail in areas where wickedness has tried to advance.

El Roi, listen to the prayers of my home. Hear our cries, our needs, our worship, and our intercession. Let Your eyes remain upon us and Your ears remain open to us. Let our family live under the canopy of divine attention and holy protection.

I declare that God sees me, hears me, and guards me. His eyes are on my life, and His ears are open to my voice. In Jesus' name, Amen.

90

Known in Every Work

> "I know your works, and your toil and perseverance, and that you can't tolerate evil men. You have tested those who call themselves apostles, and they are not, and found them false. You have perseverance and have endured for my name's sake, and have not grown weary."
> — Revelation 2:2–3 WEB

Devotional Insight

El Roi is the God who sees your labor, your endurance, your battles, and your faithfulness. Nothing you do for Him is invisible or forgotten. He sees your efforts when others don't, your perseverance when others misunderstand, and your endurance when others ignore it. This Scripture reminds the believer that God is fully aware of your toil—the sacrifices you make, the spiritual battles you fight, and the righteousness you uphold. El Roi sees your steadfastness, strengthens your resolve, and honors your perseverance.

Prayer

El Roi, God who knows my works and sees my endurance, I thank You for noticing every sacrifice I have made for Your name. You see the battles I fight, the temptations I resist, the faith I uphold, and the perseverance I cling to. Thank You for acknowledging what others overlook.

Lord, strengthen me where weariness threatens to settle. Renew my endurance. Revive my zeal. Restore my joy in serving You. Let every act of obedience be fueled by love, not obligation. Let every sacrifice be sustained by grace, not striving.

Father, You know the evil I have refused to tolerate and the truth I have defended. Continue to purify my discernment. Help me to reject deception, identify falsehood, and stand firmly in Your Word. Let my perseverance bring glory to You and advancement to Your kingdom.

El Roi, look upon my family and see our labor for Your name. Strengthen our collective perseverance. Reward our steadfastness. Honor every hidden act of faithfulness and pour fresh grace upon us to continue in righteousness without growing weary.

I declare that my works are known, my endurance is seen, and my faithfulness is valued by the God who watches over me. In Jesus' name, Amen.

PRAYERSCRIPTS

The Supreme God

אֵל גִּבּוֹר

EL GIBBOR
The Mighty God

Prayers to Call Upon the Warrior-King Who Never Loses

CYRIL OPOKU

Preface to Book 8

"Those who know your name will put their trust in you, for you, Yahweh, have not forsaken those who seek you."
— Psalms 9:10 (WEB)

There is a kind of trust that is forged not in comfort, but in conflict—a confidence that rises when the Name of God is known not merely as doctrine, but as deliverance. Psalm 9:10 anchors this final book of Part 1 with a powerful assurance: those who know God's Name discover that He never abandons those who seek Him. This truth finds its bold and triumphant expression in *Book 8—* **EL GIBBOR: *The Mighty God.*** To know God as **El Gibbor** is to trust Him as the Divine Warrior, the undefeated Champion, the Mighty Hero who enters the battle on behalf of His people.

Throughout Scripture, El Gibbor is revealed as the God who fights for His own—not with uncertainty or hesitation, but with irresistible strength and guaranteed victory. He is not startled by opposition nor intimidated by enemies. He confronts injustice, breaks strongholds, and overturns threats that are impossible by human strength alone. Psalm 9:10 assures us that those who seek Him are not forsaken, and El Gibbor is the embodiment of that promise in action. When God shows Himself strong, it is proof that He has not withdrawn, not ignored, and not abandoned His people in their moment of need.

This book invites you to trust God in the face of battle—whether spiritual, emotional, relational, or circumstantial. El Gibbor does not merely comfort; He contends. He does not only reassure; He rescues. As you move through these prayers, may the revelation of His might replace fear with courage, despair with hope, and weakness with strength. To know His Name is to stand confidently, knowing that the Mighty God has not forsaken you—and never will.

To the Praise of His Name!
Cyril O.
(Illinois | December 2025)

Introduction to Book 8

Every believer eventually encounters a battle they cannot win by strength, strategy, or experience alone.

EL GIBBOR: *The Mighty God* brings you face-to-face with the God who never loses a battle and never abandons His people in the fight. El Gibbor is the Warrior-King who rises on behalf of those who seek Him, confronting what threatens them and securing victory where defeat once seemed inevitable. When you know God by this Name, trust becomes bold, prayer becomes confident, and faith becomes fearless—not because the battle disappears, but because the outcome is no longer in doubt.

This book concludes **Part 1 (Books 1–8)** of *The Supreme God* series, following the revelations of Elohim, Yahweh, Adonai, El Elyon, El Shaddai, El Olam, and El Roi. Having encountered God as Creator, Eternal I AM, Master, Most High, Almighty, Everlasting, and All-Seeing, you now meet Him as the Mighty God who secures victory. From here, you are invited to continue into **Part 2 (Books 9–16)**, where the revelation expands into God's glory, truth, knowledge, holiness, life, heavenly dominion, and kingship.

As you begin this book, may your faith rise to meet the God who fights for you—and may you trust Him fully as El Gibbor, the Mighty God.

91

Triumph Born of Majesty

"For to us a child is born. To us a son is given; and the government will be on his shoulders. His name will be called Wonderful Counselor, Mighty God, Everlasting Father, Prince of Peace."

— Isaiah 9:6 (WEB)

Devotional Insight

El Gibbor—"Mighty God"—reveals Jesus as the divine warrior whose strength is unmatched and whose dominion is absolute. In this prophetic declaration, the Child born and Son given carries all rule, power, and government upon His shoulders. For the believer, this means that no battle begins with our weakness but with His eternal might. His counsel directs our steps, His fatherly care holds our hearts, His peace steadies our souls, and His might secures our victory. El Gibbor fights for us not from afar but from within us, empowering us to stand, overcome, and triumph. Today, the Mighty God manifests in every place you feel small, overwhelmed, or outmatched—reminding you that your life is governed by the strength of the One who cannot be defeated.

Prayer

Mighty God, I exalt You today as the Warrior King who reigns over every realm of my life. You are the Child given yet the eternal Champion who stands unmatched in power and unchallenged in authority. I honor You as the One who carries the government of my life upon Your shoulders, breaking every false dominion that has tried to assert itself against me and my family.

O El Gibbor, rise within me today. Let Your mighty strength swallow my fears, silence my anxieties, and overturn every verdict spoken by darkness. Where the enemy has tried to magnify his threats, magnify Your glory. Where weakness has whispered discouragement, let Your power thunder with hope. Be my Wonderful Counselor in decisions, my Everlasting Father in identity, my Prince of Peace in storms.

Lord, fight for my household as the Mighty God who never loses. Break cycles, lift burdens, collapse barriers, and overthrow spiritual resistance. Let my life demonstrate that my strength does not come from human might, but from the One whose name is victory itself.

Jesus, Mighty God, be enthroned in every battle, every choice, every day. Let Your supremacy write my story and Your dominion secure my destiny.

In Your name I pray, Amen.

92

The Warrior of My Salvation

"Yah is my strength and song. He has become my salvation. This is my God, and I will praise him; my father's God, and I will exalt him. Yahweh is a man of war. Yahweh is his name."

— Exodus 15:2–3 (WEB)

Devotional Insight

El Gibbor shines through this victory song as the God who becomes our strength, not just the giver of it. He enters our battles as the divine warrior whose presence brings salvation and whose might establishes triumph. For believers today, this Name means God is not distant from your warfare—He steps into it with warrior intention and covenant loyalty. He is the One who fights for your freedom, dismantles your enemies, and leads you into victory you could never secure on your own. When you face overwhelming odds, El Gibbor declares that deliverance is His specialty. He does not call you to fight alone; He fights *through* you, *for* you, and *ahead* of you. His warfare identity becomes your confidence in every struggle.

Prayer

Yahweh, Man of War, I lift my voice in praise to You—the God who steps into my battles with unstoppable might. I worship You as my strength, my song, and my salvation. You are not only the God of my fathers but the Champion of my present and the Defender of my future. Where I feel weak, You arise strong. Where I feel overwhelmed, You become my victory.

O El Gibbor, wage war over every place of contention in my life. Fight for my peace, for my family, for my destiny, and for every promise You have spoken concerning me. Let every enemy that lifts itself against Your purposes collapse under the weight of Your glory. Let the roar of Your triumph drown out the echoes of defeat that have tried to shape my thoughts.

Lord, march into every battlefront of my life. Bring deliverance where bondage tried to root itself. Bring breakthrough where resistance has been long-standing. Bring salvation where despair tried to settle. You are Yahweh, the Man of War—let every adversary know that I am defended by the Mighty One.

I praise You because the war is Yours, the power is Yours, and the victory belongs to Your name. In Jesus' name, Amen.

93

Stand Still and See Victory

"Moses said to the people, 'Don't be afraid. Stand still, and see the salvation of Yahweh, which he will work for you today; for the Egyptians whom you have seen today, you shall never see again. Yahweh will fight for you, and you shall be still.'"

— Exodus 14:13–14 (WEB)

Devotional Insight

El Gibbor reveals Himself as the God who commands victory even when you feel powerless. Israel stood trapped between an uncrossable sea and an unstoppable army, yet the Mighty God declared that fear would not decide their future—His salvation would. For believers, this Name assures us that divine intervention is not a story of the past but a present reality. El Gibbor invites you to cease striving, silence panic, and watch Him accomplish what human strength cannot. When you face impossible pressures, He stands as your Warrior—fighting, shielding, and delivering you with authority that cannot be contested. Stillness becomes strength when the Mighty God is fighting for you.

Prayer

El Gibbor, Mighty Warrior, I come before You acknowledging that there are battles too heavy for me, pressures too great, and paths too unclear. Yet You are the God who commands me not to fear. You invite me to stand still and behold Your salvation. Today I yield every frantic part of my heart to Your conquering peace.

Lord, fight for me. Where enemies have gathered around my progress, scatter them. Where obstacles have hemmed me in, break open the waters. Where fear has tried to dictate my decisions, let Your presence stabilize my soul. I trust in the God who defeats what threatens me and silences what intimidates me.

El Gibbor, let my eyes witness Your saving power. Remove the Egyptians of my past—bondage, failure, shame, accusation—and let them be seen no more. Establish a new beginning where the enemy expects an ending. Release Your warrior angels over my household, my work, my calling, and my destiny.

I choose stillness—not as surrender to defeat but as confidence in the Mighty God who fights on my behalf. Lord, let Your victory manifest in ways that leave no doubt that You alone are God. In Jesus' name, Amen.

94

He Fights Before Me

"Yahweh your God who goes before you, he will fight for you, according to all that he did for you in Egypt before your eyes."

— Deuteronomy 1:30 (WEB)

Devotional Insight

El Gibbor is the God who goes *before* you—never behind, never absent, never late. In this revelation, God reminds His people that every new challenge is already conquered by His previous faithfulness. The same Warrior who broke Egypt's power fights for His children in every season. For believers, this means your battles are never entered alone; the Mighty God precedes you, clearing the path, confronting opposition, and setting victory in motion before you ever arrive. When fear whispers that you are unprepared, El Gibbor answers: *"I am already ahead of you."* His past works anchor present confidence and strengthen future hope.

Prayer

El Gibbor, the God who goes before me, I honor You today as my divine Forerunner and unconquerable Warrior. You do not wait for me to arrive at the battlefield—you step into it ahead of me, securing the victory before the conflict even touches my life. I praise You for being the God who fights for me with a faithfulness that never weakens.

Lord, go before my family, before my assignments, before my steps, and before my future. Confront what I cannot see. Overthrow what was designed to obstruct me. Disarm what was crafted to intimidate me. As You did in Egypt, demonstrate Your power again in my life—open doors no one can close and close the doors no enemy can reopen.

Mighty God, I refuse to fear the unknown because You dwell in it. I refuse to be paralyzed by potential threats because You have already addressed them. Walk before me into every conversation, every opportunity, every challenge, and every decision. Let the footprint of Your power be visible in every outcome.

Strengthen me to follow where You lead and to rest in the assurance that Your victory surrounds me. You are the God who has gone before me, is with me, and will sustain me. In Jesus' name, Amen.

95

The God Who Fights for Me

"When you go out to battle against your enemies, and see horses, chariots, and a people more numerous than you, don't be afraid of them; for Yahweh your God, who brought you up out of the land of Egypt, is with you... For Yahweh your God is he who goes with you, to fight for you against your enemies, to save you."

— Deuteronomy 20:1–4 (WEB)

Devotional Insight

El Gibbor reveals that God's presence, not the absence of intimidating circumstances, is what guarantees victory. He does not promise that battles will look small—He promises that He is bigger. The Mighty God fights for His people with covenant love and unstoppable strength. For believers today, this means that no opposition—whether spiritual, emotional, relational, or circumstantial—can overpower the God who wars on your behalf. His presence turns fear into courage and impossibility into deliverance. El Gibbor does not merely inspire you; He saves you with His own arm.

Prayer

El Gibbor, Mighty Warrior, I acknowledge today that the battles before me are not mine—they are Yours. When I look at the size of what opposes me, fear tries to rise, but You remind me that Your presence outweighs every threat. You are the God who brought me out of past bondages, and You will save me again in the present.

Lord, fight for me. Fight for my breakthroughs, for my household, for my health, for my future, and for every promise that You have spoken. Where the enemy shows horses and chariots—intimidation, pressure, delay, or resistance—let Your might arise and scatter them. Let nothing exalt itself above Your saving power.

Go with me into every arena of life. Let Your strength overshadow my weakness. Let Your courage rise in my spirit. Let Your salvation manifest in undeniable ways. I do not enter any battle alone—I march with the Mighty God who delivers.

El Gibbor, save me where I cannot save myself. Fight for me where I cannot fight. Let every outcome testify that my victory is rooted in Your strength, not my ability. In Jesus' name, Amen.

96

One Can Chase a Thousand

"One man of you shall chase a thousand; for it is Yahweh your God who fights for you, as he spoke to you."

— Joshua 23:10 (WEB)

Devotional Insight

El Gibbor empowers His people with supernatural capability far beyond natural strength. Israel was reminded that their victories never depended on their numbers but on the Mighty God who fought for them. Today, this Name assures every believer that with God's strength, you are never the weaker side of the battle. El Gibbor multiplies your effectiveness, magnifies your impact, and neutralizes the power of opposing forces. When you feel outnumbered, God's might becomes your advantage. When you feel insufficient, His strength becomes your confidence. El Gibbor makes one person—fully yielded to Him—unstoppable against a thousand adversaries. Victory is never about your size; it is about your God.

Prayer

Mighty God, El Gibbor, I worship You as the Strength who makes me mighty in battle. You are the God who transforms weakness into boldness and smallness into supernatural influence. I acknowledge that without You I can do nothing, but with You one can chase a thousand, and a thousand can collapse before the strength You release through Your people.

Lord, let Your power rise within me today. Give me the courage to face everything that has opposed my advancement. Let me not measure myself by the size of my challenge but by the greatness of the God who fights for me. Every enemy that outnumbers me—spiritually, financially, emotionally, or circumstantially—bows to Your might.

Father, infuse my household with this same supernatural empowerment. Let every member of my family walk in the boldness of those who know God fights for them. Break off fear, anxiety, and inferiority. Replace them with confidence rooted in Your presence and strength.

El Gibbor, let my life demonstrate that You are the God who multiplies capacity. Give me victory that makes no sense to the natural eye. Let the testimony of my life be this: "Yahweh fought for me." In Jesus' name, Amen.

97

The Lord Is With You, Mighty Warrior

"Yahweh's angel appeared to him, and said to him, 'Yahweh is with you, you mighty man of valor!'"

— Judges 6:12 (WEB)

Devotional Insight

El Gibbor calls out strength where we only see weakness. Gideon felt insignificant, fearful, and inadequate, yet God addressed him according to divine identity, not human insecurity. The Mighty God sees what He placed within you long before you feel capable of walking in it. As a believer, you carry the presence of El Gibbor, which means your battles are not fought alone and your identity is not defined by your fears. God transforms ordinary people into mighty warriors by the power of His presence. He speaks courage into trembling hearts and awakens divine valor where defeat once lived.

Prayer

Lord, El Gibbor, I receive Your declaration over my life today: "Yahweh is with you, mighty warrior." Even when I feel small, You call me strong. Even when I feel overlooked, You call me chosen. Even when I feel unqualified, You call me equipped. I thank You that Your presence defines who I am—not my past, not my fears, not my limitations.

God of valor, rise within me. Awaken every dormant gift, every buried courage, every silenced strength. Let the warrior You see in me come alive by the breath of Your Spirit. Uproot every lie that tells me I am too weak, too flawed, or too insignificant for Your purposes.

El Gibbor, stand with me in every assignment You have given. Let Your courage clothe my mind, Your strength steady my heart, and Your power guide my steps. Teach me to see myself through the eyes of the Mighty God who calls things that are not as though they were.

Lord, do for me what You did for Gideon: transform my fear into faith, my hiding into rising, my trembling into triumph. Let every battle become the platform where Your strength is revealed in me. In Jesus' name, Amen.

98

The God of My Deliverance

"'Then David said to the Philistine, "You come to me with a sword, with a spear, and with a javelin; but I come to you in the name of Yahweh of Armies, the God of the armies of Israel, whom you have defied... that all this assembly may know that Yahweh doesn't save with sword and spear; for the battle is Yahweh's, and he will give you into our hand."'"

— 1 Samuel 17:45–47 (WEB)

Devotional Insight

El Gibbor reveals that victory is not achieved through human weapons but through the power of God's name. When David confronted Goliath, he stood not in physical strength but in divine authority. For believers, the Mighty God still empowers those who feel outmatched or underestimated. When you face giants—intimidating problems, spiritual resistance, overwhelming odds—El Gibbor fights through you. He turns ordinary obedience into extraordinary triumphs. Your confidence is never in what you carry but in the One whose name you represent. The battle belongs to the Lord, and His victory becomes your inheritance.

Prayer

El Gibbor, Yahweh of Armies, I come before You today not with the weapons of human strength but in the power of Your name. You are the God who brings down giants, overturns threats, and silences every voice that defies Your purpose in my life. I refuse to measure my challenges by their size; I measure them by Your majesty.

Lord, every Goliath standing before me—fear, financial pressure, spiritual warfare, generational patterns, delays—falls before the power of Your presence. I declare that the battle is Yours. You fight for me, You empower me, and You give me victory that testifies of Your greatness.

Strengthen my heart like David's. Let boldness rise where intimidation once ruled. Teach me to speak with the authority of one who knows the Mighty God stands behind every word of faith. Let my life be a demonstration that You save not by human means but by divine power.

O Warrior King, give me the courage to run toward what once terrified me. Let every victory You win through me bring glory to Your name and liberation to those connected to my destiny. In Jesus' name, Amen.

99

My Rock and Fortress

"'He said, "Yahweh is my rock, my fortress, and my deliverer, even mine; God is my rock in whom I take refuge, my shield, and the horn of my salvation, my high tower, and my refuge. My savior, you save me from violence. I call on Yahweh, who is worthy to be praised; So shall I be saved from my enemies.""'

— 2 Samuel 22:2–4 (WEB)

Devotional Insight

El Gibbor is not only a warrior who fights your battles—He is the fortress who shelters you during them. David's declaration reveals a Mighty God who defends, shields, delivers, and preserves His people. As a believer, you stand wrapped in the strength of a God who cannot be shaken. When life feels unstable, He is your rock. When opposition rises, He is your fortress. When attacks intensify, He is your shield. El Gibbor surrounds you with protection that no force of darkness can penetrate. His might is not only offensive in battle but defensive in refuge.

Prayer

El Gibbor, my Rock and Fortress, I honor You today as my unwavering defense. When the ground beneath me shifts, You remain steady. When danger circles, You encompass me with salvation. You are my shield, my refuge, my stronghold, and my deliverer. In You alone do I place my trust.

Lord, cover my life in Your strength. Let Your fortress surround my family. Let Your shield guard my mind, my health, my finances, my purpose, and every place You have called me to build. Be the horn of salvation that breaks every assault of the enemy and the tower that lifts me above every storm.

When fear tries to whisper, remind me that I am hidden in the Mighty God. When the enemy attempts to intimidate, remind me that no attack can penetrate the refuge of Your presence. You are not only the God who saves me—you are the place where I am safe.

El Gibbor, arise and scatter anything that seeks to violate my peace. Strengthen my spirit to remain anchored in You. Let my testimony echo David's: "I called on Yahweh, and I was saved from my enemies." In Jesus' name, Amen.

100

Rescued by His Power

"Yahweh is my rock, my fortress, and my deliverer; my God, my rock, in whom I will take refuge; my shield, and the horn of my salvation, my high tower. I call on Yahweh, who is worthy to be praised; and I am saved from my enemies. The cords of death surrounded me. The floods of ungodliness made me afraid. The cords of Sheol were around me. The snares of death came on me. In my distress I called on Yahweh, and cried to my God. He heard my voice out of his temple. My cry before him came into his ears. Then the earth shook and trembled. The foundations also of the mountains quaked and were shaken, because he was angry."

— Psalm 18:2–7 (WEB) *(Note: Psalm 18:2–17 will be used across the next prayers as required.)*

Devotional Insight

El Gibbor is the God who responds to your cry with earth-shaking power. In this passage, David describes a Mighty God who does not observe distress from afar—He intervenes with fierce and passionate deliverance. When the enemy surrounds you with fear, darkness, or pressure, El Gibbor rises in holy anger to rescue you. Your cries do not fall into silence; they enter the ears of the God who acts. As a believer, you are never abandoned in struggle. The Mighty God shakes foundations, breaks snares, and dismantles every weapon formed against you. His strength is your salvation, and His passion is your protection.

Prayer

El Gibbor, Mighty Rescuer, I thank You that my cries never go unheard. When I call, You answer. When I am overwhelmed, You arise. When darkness presses in, Your light breaks through with unstoppable force. You are the God who shakes the earth on behalf of Your children.

Lord, every fear that has attempted to surround me—scatter it by Your might. Every trap set against my destiny—break it open. Every voice of death, defeat, or despair—silence it with Your life-giving power. You are my Rock, my Fortress, my Deliverer, my High Tower. I hide in You, and I am safe.

Father, hear my cry today and move with the passion of Psalm 18. Let the earth shake in the spirit realm. Let foundations built by the enemy crumble. Let every demonic assignment be overturned by Your righteous anger. Fight for my family, my calling, my future, and every promise written over my life.

I praise You because salvation belongs to You. Victory belongs to You. Deliverance belongs to You. And because I belong to You, these triumphs become my inheritance. In Jesus' name, Amen.

101

The King of Glory in Battle

"Lift up your heads, you gates! Be lifted up, you everlasting doors, and the King of glory will come in. Who is the King of glory? Yahweh strong and mighty, Yahweh mighty in battle. Lift up your heads, you gates! Yes, lift them up, you everlasting doors, and the King of glory will come in. Who is this King of glory? Yahweh of Armies is the King of glory."

— Psalm 24:7–10 (WEB)

Devotional Insight

El Gibbor is revealed as the King of Glory who enters every battle with undefeatable strength. When the psalm commands gates to lift their heads, it signifies the surrender of every barrier, hindrance, and resistance to the arrival of the Mighty God. For the believer, this means that every place in your life that feels shut, blocked, or locked is commanded to open when El Gibbor draws near. He does not slip into your situation quietly—He enters as Yahweh strong and mighty, the One who conquers what confronts you. When you welcome His presence, you welcome victory. When the King of Glory comes in, no enemy can remain standing.

Prayer

King of Glory, El Gibbor, I open the gates of my heart, my home, my future, and every battle I face. Come in with Your strength. Come in with Your power. Come in as the Mighty One who never loses. I lift up the ancient doors of my destiny that have been shut, and I declare: the King of Glory enters now.

Yahweh strong and mighty, overthrow everything that has exalted itself against Your purpose in my life. Let every barrier lift. Let every gate yield. Let every spiritual obstruction bow to Your authority. Arise in Your majesty and reveal Yourself as the God mighty in battle.

Fight for my family today. Fight for our breakthroughs, our health, our progress, and our peace. Drive out the enemy with the force of Your presence. Let every demonic gate slam shut, and every heavenly gate swing wide. Let Your glory fill every place where darkness attempted to reign.

Yahweh of Armies, be enthroned over my circumstances. March as King over every area of my life. Let the testimony of my home, my calling, and my journey be this: The King of Glory came in, and victory followed. In Jesus' name, Amen.

102

Fearless in the Face of Battle

"Yahweh is my light and my salvation. Whom shall I fear? Yahweh is the strength of my life. Of whom shall I be afraid? When evildoers came at me to eat up my flesh, even my adversaries and my foes, they stumbled and fell. Though an army should encamp against me, my heart shall not fear. Though war should rise against me, even then I will be confident."

— Psalm 27:1-3 (WEB)

Devotional Insight

El Gibbor destroys fear by revealing Himself as your light, salvation, and strength. David's confidence was not rooted in self-assurance but in the presence of the Mighty God who stood as his defender. When El Gibbor is your strength, intimidation loses its grip. Armies may gather, opposition may intensify, and warfare may rise, but the believer who trusts in the Mighty God stands unshaken. God's light exposes danger, His salvation delivers from threats, and His strength empowers endurance. Fear cannot coexist with the presence of El Gibbor—His courage becomes your confidence.

Prayer

El Gibbor, Mighty God, You are my light when darkness tries to overwhelm me. You are my salvation when danger rises. You are my strength when my heart feels faint. Today I stand in the truth that with You, I have nothing to fear. No adversary, no threat, no warfare, no opposition can undo what You have established in my life.

Lord, when evildoers rise against me, let them stumble and fall by the power of Your presence. When spiritual armies encamp around my destiny, let my heart remain untroubled, anchored in the strength of the Mighty God. You are the confidence of my soul and the fortress of my life.

Silence every whisper of fear. Break the grip of anxiety. Uproot every internal trembling. Flood my spirit with the boldness of one who walks with the God of all power. Let courage rise like fire within me and let every thought align with Your victory.

Yahweh, strengthen my family with this same fearless confidence. Let no threat intimidate us. Let no battle shake us. Let no enemy prevail over us. Surround us with the assurance that El Gibbor fights for us, stands with us, and leads us into triumph. In Jesus' name, Amen.

103

Your Right Hand Has Saved Us

"We have heard with our ears, God; our fathers have told us what work you did in their days, in the days of old. You drove out the nations with your hand, but you planted them. You afflicted the peoples, but you spread them abroad. For they didn't get the land in possession by their own sword, neither did their own arm save them; but your right hand, your arm, and the light of your face, because you were favorable to them... For I will not trust in my bow, neither shall my sword save me. But you have saved us from our adversaries, and have shamed those who hate us. In God we have made our boast all day long, and we will give thanks to your name forever."

— Psalm 44:1–8 (WEB)

Devotional Insight

El Gibbor is the God whose victories transcend human ability. Israel learned that their triumphs came not from their swords but from God's arm and His favor. For believers today, this passage teaches that true breakthrough flows not from personal strength, strategy, or skill, but from the Mighty God who fights on your behalf. El Gibbor saves, delivers, plants, establishes, and expands His people by His own power. When you boast, you boast in Him. When you advance, you advance by His favor. His mighty hand secures what your own hand never could.

Prayer

El Gibbor, Mighty Warrior, I thank You for every victory You have given—not one of them came from my strength but from Your arm. You are the God who drives out enemies, establishes Your people, spreads them abroad, and secures what no human power can hold. Today I acknowledge that my life is built on Your victories, not my abilities.

Lord, let Your right hand work powerfully in my life again. Where doors have resisted, open them. Where enemies have encamped, scatter them. Where progress has been hindered, advance me by Your favor. I renounce trust in human strength, human plans, or human efforts. My boast is in the Mighty God alone.

Fight for my family. Save us from adversaries seen and unseen. Let every weapon formed against us fail by the brilliance of Your light. Shame every force that hates Your purpose for our lives. Lift our heads and expand our borders by the power of Your favor.

El Gibbor, write new testimonies in my life—stories future generations will speak of, declaring, "This was the work of the Lord." Let Your name be praised forever in my home. In Jesus' name, Amen.

104

The Warrior Who Breaks Bows

"In Judah, God is known. His name is great in Israel. His tabernacle is also in Salem; his dwelling place in Zion. There he broke the flaming arrows of the bow, the shield, and the sword, and the weapons of war."

— Psalm 76:1–3 (WEB)

Devotional Insight

El Gibbor is the God who disarms the enemy before the battle ever reaches you. In Zion, God shattered weapons designed to destroy His people. For the believer, this reveals a profound truth: the Mighty God breaks the power of attacks before they manifest. Flaming arrows are extinguished, shields and swords lose their force, and warfare is neutralized in His presence. You do not live at the mercy of the enemy's weapons. You live under the protection of the God who renders them powerless. El Gibbor is known through His acts of deliverance, and His dwelling among His people ensures supernatural defense.

Prayer

El Gibbor, God of Zion, I exalt You as the Mighty One who neutralizes every weapon formed against Your children. Your name is great, Your presence mighty, and Your deliverance unmatched. I thank You that You do not merely defend me in battle—You destroy the enemy's weapons before they can touch my life.

Lord, break every flaming arrow aimed at my mind, my peace, my family, my progress, or my calling. Shatter every shield the enemy hides behind. Crush every sword lifted against my destiny. Let every strategy of darkness collapse in Your presence.

Establish Your dwelling in my home, my work, and my heart. Let Your nearness be my fortress. Let Your presence be my protection. Let Your greatness be seen through the downfall of every attack sent against me.

Mighty God, rise in holy power and make my life a place where weapons fail, schemes scatter, and adversaries retreat. Let every spiritual assault dissolve before it ever reaches me, because El Gibbor is here. In Jesus' name, Amen.

105

The God Who Rules the Seas

"Yahweh, God of Armies, who is a mighty one, like you? Yah, your faithfulness is around you. You rule the pride of the sea. When its waves rise up, you calm them. You have broken Rahab in pieces, like one of the slain. You have scattered your enemies with your mighty arm."

— Psalm 89:8–10 (WEB)

Devotional Insight

El Gibbor is unmatched in might and unrivaled in authority. This passage reveals His supremacy over creation, chaos, and enemies alike. The sea represents instability, turmoil, and overwhelming circumstances—yet God rules it with ease. Rahab symbolizes fierce spiritual opposition—yet God shatters it without effort. For the believer, El Gibbor stands as the Mighty God who calms what rages, breaks what resists, and scatters what threatens. His faithfulness surrounds you like a shield, assuring you that no storm or enemy can overpower His arm.

Prayer

El Gibbor, Yahweh of Armies, there is none mighty like You. You are the God who stands above storms, above chaos, above every rising wave of circumstance. When life surges, You calm it. When enemies rise, You scatter them. When opposition forms itself like Rahab, You break it to pieces by the strength of Your arm.

Mighty God, speak to every storm in my life—calm the waves that threaten my peace. Silence the winds that war against my progress. Establish divine order where chaos has attempted to reign. Let the authority of Your voice drown out the noise of fear, anxiety, and confusion.

Lord, break every Rahab—every spiritual resistance, demonic assignment, generational stronghold, and adversarial force standing against my destiny. Shatter them by Your power. Scatter them by Your arm. Let nothing prevail against the purposes You have spoken over my life.

Surround me with Your faithfulness. Wrap my home, my family, my work, my health, and my future in the strength of Your covenant love. Let every rising wave bow to El Gibbor—the Mighty God who rules the seas. In Jesus' name, Amen.

106

Mountains Melt Before Him

"Yahweh reigns! Let the earth rejoice! Let the multitude of islands be glad! Clouds and darkness are around him. Righteousness and justice are the foundation of his throne. A fire goes before him, and burns up his adversaries on every side. His lightning lights up the world. The earth sees, and trembles. The mountains melt like wax at the presence of Yahweh, at the presence of the Lord of the whole earth."

— Psalm 97:1–5 (WEB)

Devotional Insight

El Gibbor is the Mighty God before whom nothing can stand—not mountains, not adversaries, not darkness, not resistance. His presence is fire that consumes opposition and light that exposes every hidden work of darkness. For the believer, this passage reveals that God's power does not merely struggle against enemies—it overwhelms them. The mountains symbolizing impossibility dissolve like wax before Him. When El Gibbor steps into your situation, what once appeared unmovable becomes powerless. His reign establishes righteousness, His presence brings trembling breakthrough, and His justice guarantees victory.

Prayer

El Gibbor, Lord of the whole earth, I honor You as the God before whom mountains melt. You reign in glory, You reign in power, You reign in justice. Let Your presence fill my life today as consuming fire and illuminating light. Where darkness tries to gather, scatter it with Your brilliance.

Mighty God, burn up every adversary rising around my destiny. Let every enemy—seen or unseen, physical or spiritual—be consumed by the fire that goes before You. Let every mountain that has stood against my progress, peace, or purpose dissolve at Your presence.

God of justice, establish Your throne in my home. Let righteousness rule over every decision, every atmosphere, every trajectory of my family. Cause the earth around me to tremble at the demonstration of Your mighty work.

El Gibbor, make my life a testimony that no obstacle can resist the presence of the Mighty God. Melt what is hardened. Break what is stubborn. Overturn what is resistant. Let the fire of Your victory go before me today. In Jesus' name, Amen.

107

Returning to the Mighty God

"A remnant will return, even the remnant of Jacob, to the mighty God."

— Isaiah 10:21 (WEB)

Devotional Insight

El Gibbor is the God to whom His people return for restoration, strength, and deliverance. Even when Israel wandered, God preserved a remnant who would come back to His power. For believers today, this Name reveals that God is not only mighty in battle but mighty in mercy. He welcomes the return of those who feel weary, distant, or overwhelmed. His might is not only for conquering enemies—it is for restoring His people to fullness. When you return to El Gibbor, you return to the One who strengthens your heart, reclaims your destiny, and realigns your path with His victory.

Prayer

El Gibbor, Mighty God, I return to You today with all my heart. Draw me into Your strength, into Your presence, and into the fullness of who You are. Where I have felt distant, restore me. Where I have felt weary, revive me. Where I have felt overwhelmed, reestablish me in Your might.

Lord, let every wandering place in my soul return to the Mighty God. Restore my fire. Renew my courage. Refresh my spirit. Let every area where I have drifted be drawn back into alignment with Your purpose. I declare that I am part of the remnant who returns—not in weakness, but in worship.

God of restoration, strengthen my family to return to You as well. Bring us back to faith, back to prayer, back to obedience, back to trust, back to divine confidence. Let every broken place become whole under Your mighty hand.

El Gibbor, I return not just for refuge, but for empowerment. Fill my life with the strength of the Mighty God. Reclaim every promise, every calling, every breakthrough that belongs to me. Establish me again in Your victory. In Jesus' name, Amen.

108

The Hero Who Marches Forth

"Yahweh will go out as a mighty man. He will stir up zeal like a man of war. He will raise a war cry. Yes, he will shout aloud. He will triumph over his enemies."

— Isaiah 42:13 (WEB)

Devotional Insight

El Gibbor is the God who does not sit passively—He rises, marches, cries out, and triumphs. Isaiah describes God not as distant but as a warrior filled with zeal, passion, and force. He does not merely watch battles unfold; He enters them with a shout that scatters darkness. For the believer, this means God is actively engaged in your warfare. His zeal fights for your deliverance, His shout breaks your oppression, and His triumph becomes your victory. When El Gibbor rises, every enemy falls.

Prayer

El Gibbor, rise in my life today. Go out as the Mighty Man, the God of war who defends His people with divine zeal. Stir Yourself like the warrior Isaiah saw—full of passion, full of fire, full of unstoppable resolve. Raise Your war cry over my battles. Let Your shout silence every voice that stands against me.

Lord, triumph over every enemy confronting my destiny. Triumph over fear, over confusion, over delay, over opposition, over spiritual resistance. Let Your shout break chains. Let Your triumph open doors. Let Your zeal pursue my deliverance until every adversary bows.

Mighty God, go forth before my family. March into every area where darkness has tried to settle. Drive out every force that resists generational blessing. Overturn every assignment of the enemy. Let Your victorious shout echo through our home, our work, our finances, and our future.

El Gibbor, triumph again and again. Let victory flow like a river. Let breakthrough fall like rain. Let Your warrior presence be the anthem of my life. In Jesus' name, Amen.

109

The Lord Is With Me as a Mighty Warrior

"But Yahweh is with me as an awesome mighty one. Therefore my persecutors will stumble, and they won't prevail. They will be utterly disappointed because they have not dealt wisely, even with an everlasting dishonor which will never be forgotten."

— Jeremiah 20:11 (WEB)

Devotional Insight

El Gibbor stands with His people as an "awesome mighty one"—fearsome to enemies, comforting to His children. Jeremiah faced persecution, pressure, and mockery, yet he declared confidence in the God who would cause his enemies to stumble. For believers, this Name assures us that opposition cannot prevail when the Mighty God stands beside us. Every adversary that rises against you will be disappointed and overthrown. El Gibbor's presence guarantees that no plot will succeed and no attack will outsmart the God who defends His own.

Prayer

El Gibbor, Mighty Warrior, thank You for standing with me as the awesome One who terrifies my enemies but strengthens my soul. Because You are with me, I fear no opposition. I stand tall, bold, and confident—not in my ability, but in Your undefeatable presence.

Lord, let every persecutor, every adversary, every spiritual attacker stumble and fail. Disappoint every strategy meant to harm me. Let the shame they intended for me return upon their own plans. Expose every hidden agenda. Overthrow every scheme. Scatter every plot that rises against my destiny.

Mighty God, surround my family with this same warrior presence. Let no attack prosper. Let no curse find its target. Let no opposition succeed. Let every force that rises against us fall—because the Mighty Warrior stands with us.

El Gibbor, let Your presence be my armor. Let Your nearness be my defense. Let Your strength be my peace. Cause every plan of darkness to collapse in everlasting dishonor while Your victory shines through my life. In Jesus' name, Amen.

110

Nothing Too Hard for the Mighty God

"Ah Lord Yahweh! Behold, you have made the heavens and the earth by your great power and by your outstretched arm. There is nothing too hard for you, who show loving kindness to thousands, and repay the iniquity of the fathers into the bosom of their children after them, the great, the mighty God, Yahweh of Armies is his name."

— Jeremiah 32:17–18 (WEB)

Devotional Insight

El Gibbor is the God of limitless power—nothing is too hard for Him. Jeremiah declares that the same God who created the heavens and earth by His outstretched arm is the Mighty God who works in the lives of His people with both justice and mercy. For the believer, this means no obstacle is too great, no bondage too strong, no need too deep, and no battle too intense for El Gibbor. His might is anchored in love and exercised through covenant faithfulness. When you face impossibilities, the Mighty God declares, "Nothing is too hard for Me."

Prayer

El Gibbor, Mighty God, I stand in awe of Your greatness. You stretched out Your arm and formed the heavens. You established the earth with a word. You hold galaxies in place and sustain creation by Your power. There is nothing too hard for You—and because You are my God, nothing in my life is beyond Your reach.

Lord, stretch out Your mighty arm over every impossibility confronting me. Break through barriers. Overturn limitations. Dissolve obstacles. Release solutions. Let every "too hard" place in my life become a testimony of Your power.

God of mercy and justice, show loving kindness to me and my family. Cover us with favor. Surround us with protection. Break generational iniquity and release generational blessing. Let the power that created the world move in my home, my work, my health, my finances, and my destiny.

El Gibbor, reveal Yourself as the Mighty God of my situation. Work wonders. Perform miracles. Demonstrate Your greatness. Let my life bear witness that Yahweh of Armies is His name and nothing is too hard for Him. In Jesus' name, Amen.

111

The Voice That Commands Armies

"Yahweh thunders his voice before his army; for his forces are very great; for he is strong who obeys his command; for the day of Yahweh is great and very awesome, and who can endure it?"

— Joel 2:11 (WEB)

Devotional Insight

El Gibbor is the Mighty God whose voice commands armies and whose strength empowers His people to obey. His authority is not passive—it shakes the heavens, mobilizes angelic forces, and brings divine order to the earth. For the believer, this passage reveals that God's voice is your greatest weapon and your greatest protection. When He speaks, darkness trembles. When He commands, victory advances. His strength not only conquers enemies but strengthens you to walk in obedience that produces breakthrough. El Gibbor's voice is not just sound—it is power, movement, and unstoppable triumph.

Prayer

El Gibbor, Mighty God, I bow before the voice that thunders above every circumstance. Your voice commands angels, dismantles darkness, and summons victory. Speak over my life today. Let Your command release alignment, order, and breakthrough in every area of my existence.

Lord, let Your army be mobilized on my behalf. Send forth angelic forces to defend, fight, and advance everything You have ordained for my household. Thunder against the enemies that threaten my peace, my progress, and my purpose. Shake the foundations of every opposition.

Strengthen me to obey Your command. Let Your might empower my steps. Let Your zeal ignite my obedience. Let Your word become the fire that drives my decisions. Where I have felt weak, make me strong. Where I have hesitated, make me bold. Where I have been weary, renew my spirit with the force of Your voice.

El Gibbor, let Your great and awesome day be seen in my life—not for judgment but for triumph. Let every place where the enemy hoped to prevail become the stage of Your victory. In Jesus' name, Amen.

112

The Jealous Warrior Who Defends His People

"Yahweh is a jealous God and avenges. Yahweh avenges and is full of wrath. Yahweh takes vengeance on his adversaries, and he maintains wrath against his enemies. Yahweh is slow to anger, and great in power, and will by no means leave the guilty unpunished. Yahweh has his way in the whirlwind and in the storm, and the clouds are the dust of his feet."

— Nahum 1:2–3 (WEB)

Devotional Insight

El Gibbor is the Mighty God whose jealousy is not insecurity—it is protective love. His wrath is not uncontrolled rage—it is justice against the forces that harm His own. He is patient, yet powerful; merciful, yet unstoppable. For the believer, this passage reveals a God who defends fiercely, avenges righteously, and moves through storms with authority. He refuses to allow evil to win. When the whirlwind rises around you, El Gibbor stands in it and commands it. His power ensures that no attack against His children goes unanswered and no injustice remains unresolved.

Prayer

El Gibbor, Mighty and Jealous God, I thank You that Your love fights for me with passion and justice. You are patient with me, yet fierce against my enemies. You defend me with a vengeance that darkness cannot withstand. Today I rest under the protection of Your holy jealousy.

Lord, rise in Your justice and avenge every attack launched against my life. Confront every adversary that has lifted itself against my destiny. Render powerless every voice that has spoken evil. Overthrow every scheme designed to harm me. Let Your wrath dismantle every plan of darkness.

Great in power, move in my storms. Walk through the whirlwind surrounding my life. Let the clouds beneath Your feet testify that no chaos is too fierce for You to command. Bring order where confusion has reigned. Bring peace where turmoil has lingered. Bring justice where wrong has been done.

Mighty God, secure my household in Your protective zeal. Let no weapon succeed, no curse stand, no accusation prevail. Fight for us until every adversary is silenced. In Jesus' name, Amen.

113

The Warrior Who Rejoices Over Me

"Yahweh, your God, is in your midst, a mighty one who will save. He will rejoice over you with joy. He will calm you in his love. He will rejoice over you with singing."

— Zephaniah 3:17 (WEB)

Devotional Insight

El Gibbor is not only the Mighty God who fights for you—He is the God who delights in you. His might saves, His love calms, and His joy sings over your life. This passage reveals a warrior-God whose strength is tender, whose power is intimate, and whose presence brings peace. For the believer, this means that God is both your defender and your delight. He stands with you in battle and surrounds you with affection. The Mighty One is not distant—He is in your midst, celebrating you, strengthening you, and calming every fear with His love.

Prayer

El Gibbor, Mighty God who saves, I receive Your presence in my midst today. Thank You that You are not far away;

You stand with me, fight for me, and rejoice over me. Your delight brings me strength. Your joy becomes my refuge. Your love calms every storm inside my soul.

Lord, save me again today—not only from danger, but from fear, doubt, stress, and heaviness. Fight for my peace. Fight for my rest. Fight for my joy. Let Your mighty hand rescue me from every internal and external battle.

God who rejoices over me, let Your singing fill the atmosphere of my home. Sing over my family. Calm us with Your love. Replace every anxiety with tranquility. Replace every fear with assurance. Let Your love-lullaby silence the noise of the enemy.

El Gibbor, let me feel the weight of Your joy. Let the sound of Your singing break chains, lift burdens, and release healing. Cover me with the victory-song of the Mighty God. In Jesus' name, Amen.

114

All Authority Belongs to the Mighty One

"Jesus came to them and spoke to them, saying, 'All authority has been given to me in heaven and on earth.'"

— Matthew 28:18 (WEB)

Devotional Insight

El Gibbor is fully revealed in Jesus, the risen Lord who holds all authority everywhere. In heaven and on earth, there is no realm, no power, no force that does not bow to Him. For the believer, this means that spiritual warfare is never a contest of equals—your Savior is enthroned above every enemy. His authority commissions your purpose, empowers your prayers, and guarantees your victory. When you stand under His authority, you stand above every attack. El Gibbor in Christ is not partial power—it is total supremacy.

Prayer

Lord Jesus, Mighty God revealed in the flesh, I bow before Your unmatched authority. All authority in heaven and earth is Yours. No enemy can oppose You. No power can rival You. No battle can outmatch You. You reign in absolute supremacy.

I come under Your authority today—my life, my decisions, my family, my future, my calling. Align everything in me with Your lordship. Break every influence not submitted to You. Uproot every lie that challenges Your dominion.

Jesus, wield Your authority over every spiritual attack. Silence demons. Crush strongholds. Overthrow the kingdom of darkness. Let Your victory saturate my atmosphere and redefine my reality. Because You have all authority, I walk in security.

Lord, release Your authority into my household. Let it govern our peace, guide our steps, protect our boundaries, and empower our assignments. Let every battle we face be won in Your name before it even begins.

El Gibbor, Mighty Christ, reign over us today with the fullness of Your victorious authority.

In Your name I pray, Amen.

115

Overcoming Through the Mighty Christ

"I have told you these things, that in me you may have peace. In the world you have oppression; but cheer up! I have overcome the world."

— John 16:33 (WEB)

Devotional Insight

El Gibbor in Christ is the Overcomer who has defeated the world's systems, pressures, and powers. Jesus does not deny that oppression exists—He declares that His victory is greater. For the believer, peace is not found in the absence of trouble but in the presence of the One who has already overcome it. You do not fight for victory; you fight from victory. El Gibbor empowers you to walk in triumph over discouragement, darkness, and demonic resistance because the Overcomer lives within you.

Prayer

Mighty Jesus, El Gibbor made manifest, I receive Your peace today. Not a fragile peace that depends on circumstances, but the unstoppable peace that flows from

Your victory over the world. You have overcome everything that tries to overwhelm me.

Lord, every oppression, every pressure, every trouble that rises around me—I declare it defeated in Your name. You overcame the world, and because I am in You, I share in that triumph. Let Your overcoming power rise in me today.

Strengthen me against discouragement. Empower me against spiritual heaviness. Lift me above anxiety and cause my heart to rest in the assurance that the Mighty God has already won. Let the reality of Your victory swallow every lie of defeat.

Jesus, let Your overcoming power fill my home. Let peace reign in every room. Let hope fill every heart. Let Your triumph silence every attack of the enemy. Because You overcame, my family will overcome. Because You prevailed, we will prevail.

El Gibbor, Overcoming King, let Your victory be made manifest in every area of my life today.

In Your name I pray, Amen.

116

More Than Conquerors Through Him

"What then shall we say about these things? If God is for us, who can be against us? He who didn't spare his own Son, but delivered him up for us all, how would he not also with him freely give us all things? Who could bring a charge against God's chosen ones? It is God who justifies. Who is he who condemns? It is Christ who died, yes rather, who was raised from the dead, who is at the right hand of God, who also makes intercession for us. Who shall separate us from the love of Christ? Could oppression, or anguish, or persecution, or famine, or nakedness, or peril, or sword?... No, in all these things, we are more than conquerors through him who loved us."

— Romans 8:31–37 (WEB)

Devotional Insight

El Gibbor is the Mighty God who not only fights for you—He positions you as more than a conqueror through Christ. Nothing can rise against you successfully, because the One who stands for you is greater than all who stand against you. Christ's death, resurrection, intercession, and love secure a victory that cannot be undone. For the believer, this means that warfare does not define you; triumph does. You do not merely survive battles—you surpass them through the power of His love. El Gibbor ensures that no accusation, no affliction, no enemy, and no circumstance can separate you from the conquering power of Christ.

Prayer

El Gibbor, Mighty God, I thank You that because You are for me, nothing can stand against me. You gave Your Son for me. You justify me. You cover me. You fight for me. And because of Your love, I am more than a conqueror.

Lord, let every charge of the enemy be silenced. Let every accusation be overturned. Let every condemning voice lose its authority. Where shame tried to attach itself, release freedom. Where fear tried to paralyze me, release courage. Where darkness tried to intimidate, release light.

Jesus, You intercede for me—let that intercession echo victory into every area of my life. Let Your love override every battle. Let Your resurrection empower my spirit. Let Your triumph define my story.

El Gibbor, make my family more than conquerors. Let Your love shield us, strengthen us, and elevate us. Let no oppression, no peril, no pressure, no famine, no spiritual assault prevail. In all these things, make us victorious through the Mighty One who loves us. In Jesus' name, Amen.

117

Pulling Down Strongholds

"For though we walk in the flesh, we don't wage war according to the flesh; for the weapons of our warfare are not of the flesh, but mighty before God to the throwing down of strongholds, throwing down imaginations and every high thing that is exalted against the knowledge of God, and bringing every thought into captivity to the obedience of Christ."

— 2 Corinthians 10:3–5 (WEB)

Devotional Insight

El Gibbor empowers believers with divine weapons—spiritual, not natural; mighty, not limited. The Mighty God equips you to tear down strongholds, demolish lies, and capture thoughts that refuse to bow to Christ. Spiritual warfare is not fought with human strength but with God's incomparable power. For the believer, this means you are not helpless against mental battles, generational patterns, or spiritual resistance. El Gibbor arms you with authority that dismantles the enemy's structures and aligns your mind with the truth.

Prayer

El Gibbor, Mighty God, I thank You that though I walk in the flesh, my warfare is empowered by Your Spirit. Your weapons are mighty—not weak, not fragile, not limited, but mighty before God to overthrow every stronghold resisting my destiny.

Lord, tear down every stronghold in my mind—fear, insecurity, lies, defeat, confusion, and every imagination that exalts itself against Your truth. Let every thought be captured and brought into obedience to Christ. Let Your power rule in my inner man.

Mighty God, overthrow every high thing that has risen against my family. Break generational strongholds. Shatter spiritual resistance. Silence lying voices. Erase false identities. Uproot demonic patterns. Let the mind of Christ be established in our home.

El Gibbor, train my hands for spiritual war. Teach me how to wield the weapons of prayer, faith, Scripture, worship, and obedience. Let Your power flow through my declarations. Let Your authority clothe my thoughts. Let Your victory manifest in my inner world and outward life. In Jesus' name, Amen.

118

Standing Strong in the Mighty Lord

"Finally, be strong in the Lord, and in the strength of his might. Put on the whole armor of God, that you may be able to stand against the wiles of the devil. For our wrestling is not against flesh and blood, but against the principalities, against the powers, against the world's rulers of the darkness of this age, and against the spiritual forces of wickedness in the heavenly places. Therefore put on the whole armor of God, that you may be able to withstand in the evil day, and having done all, to stand."

— Ephesians 6:10–13 (WEB)

Devotional Insight

El Gibbor is the God whose strength clothes His people like armor. He invites you not to stand in your strength but in His. The battles you face are spiritual, but so is the power that equips you. For the believer, this passage reveals that victory comes from divine empowerment, not human effort. The Mighty God enables you to stand firm, equipped, protected, and unshaken—even in the evil day. His armor is not symbolic; it is supernatural covering. El Gibbor makes you unmovable.

Prayer

El Gibbor, Mighty Lord, I stand today in the strength of Your might—not my own. I put on the whole armor of God that You provide: truth around my waist, righteousness upon my chest, peace guiding my steps, faith shielding me, salvation guarding my mind, and the sword of the Spirit empowering my declarations.

Lord, strengthen me to stand against every scheme, trap, and ambush of the enemy. Let no deception prevail. Let no hidden agenda succeed. Let no spiritual force overpower the armor of the Mighty God that covers me.

Teach me to war not in flesh but in the Spirit. Let discernment sharpen me. Let boldness steady me. Let Your armor secure me. In the evil day, make me unshakable. When the enemy presses, keep me standing. When the winds blow, anchor me deep in Your strength.

El Gibbor, clothe my family in Your armor. Guard our minds, shield our faith, strengthen our steps, and fortify our peace. Let every attack meet the impenetrable strength of the Mighty God. In Jesus' name, Amen.

119

Greater Is He Within Me

"You are of God, little children, and have overcome them; because greater is he who is in you than he who is in the world."

— 1 John 4:4 (WEB)

Devotional Insight

El Gibbor is not only the God who fights *for* you—He is the Mighty One who lives *within* you. His indwelling presence makes you an overcomer before the battle even begins. The One inside you is greater than every demonic force, every worldly influence, and every opposing power. For the believer, this means that victory is your identity, not your ambition. You overcome because the Overcomer inhabits you. El Gibbor within you is the unstoppable force that ensures triumph over every adversary.

Prayer

El Gibbor, Mighty God within me, I thank You that Your indwelling presence is greater than anything that rises against me. You are not a distant help—you reside in my spirit. You empower me, strengthen me, defend me, and cause me to overcome.

Lord, let the revelation of "greater is He" fill every part of my mind. Let this truth silence fear, drown out lies, and break intimidation. Let every inward weakness bow to the strength of the Mighty God living inside me.

Greater are You within me than every spiritual force in the world. Greater are You within my family than every attack against our home. Greater are You within my purpose than every barrier trying to oppose it. Your greatness overwhelms every enemy.

El Gibbor, rise within me today. Overflow from my spirit into my thoughts, my emotions, my decisions, and my environment. Let the greatness of Your presence manifest in power, authority, and victory. In Jesus' name, Amen.

120

The Rider on the White Horse

"I saw the heaven opened, and behold, a white horse, and he who sat on it is called Faithful and True. In righteousness he judges and makes war. His eyes are a flame of fire, and on his head are many crowns. He has names written and a name written which no one knows but he himself. He is clothed in a garment sprinkled with blood. His name is called 'The Word of God.' The armies which are in heaven followed him on white horses, clothed in white, pure, fine linen. Out of his mouth proceeds a sharp sword, that with it he should strike the nations. He will rule them with an iron rod. He treads the wine press of the fierceness of the wrath of God, the Almighty. He has on his garment and on his thigh a name written, 'KING OF KINGS, AND LORD OF LORDS.'"

— Revelation 19:11–16 (WEB)

Devotional Insight

El Gibbor reaches His ultimate revelation in Christ, the Warrior-King who returns in glory, fire, and righteousness. Jesus appears not as the suffering Lamb but as the conquering Rider, executing judgment, defeating evil, and establishing His eternal reign. For the believer, this vision reveals the unstoppable majesty of the Mighty God. Every enemy will bow. Every force of darkness will be crushed. Every battle will end in His triumph. You belong to the Kingdom of the Warrior-King whose victory is absolute and eternal.

Prayer

El Gibbor, Faithful and True, I worship You as the Rider on the white horse—the One who judges with righteousness and wars with holy fire. Your eyes burn with truth. Your crowns proclaim Your authority. Your sword declares Your victory. You are the Mighty God who cannot be resisted, opposed, or overthrown.

Lord Jesus, King of kings and Lord of lords, reveal Your warrior majesty in my life today. Strike down every force that rises against Your purpose for me. Cut through every oppression with the sword of Your Word. Rule in my heart with the rod of Your authority. Let every enemy of my destiny bow before Your greatness.

Lead the armies of heaven over my household. Ride into every battle we face. Execute judgment on every demonic assignment. Tread down every spiritual adversary. Let Your victory fill our story.

El Gibbor, Warrior-King, be enthroned over my life. Let Your fire purify me. Let Your truth anchor me. Let Your reign govern me.

In Your name, KING OF KINGS AND LORD OF LORDS, I pray, Amen.

Epilogue

As you close this print volume of **Books 5–8**, may you recognize how your understanding of God has quietly but profoundly deepened. You have not only learned more about His Names—you have encountered how those Names meet real needs, carry real burdens, and secure real victories. God has revealed Himself here as sufficient when you are weak, constant when time stretches long, attentive when you feel unseen, and mighty when opposition rises.

What remains with you now is a strengthened confidence. You have seen that faith is not sustained by effort alone, but by encounter. The God who is All-Sufficient has met your lack. The Everlasting God has steadied your seasons. The God Who Sees has assured you of His care. The Mighty God has reminded you that you are not fighting alone. These truths are meant to walk with you beyond this book—shaping how you pray, how you endure, and how you trust.

Let Psalm 9:10 continue to echo in your heart. You know His Name more deeply now—not only as truth to believe, but as reality to live by. And because you know His Name, trust has grown stronger. The God you have sought has not forsaken you. He has revealed Himself in ways that sustain faith for the long journey.

If your heart desires to revisit the foundations that support this lived trust, the companion print collection featuring **Books 1–4** awaits—anchoring faith once again in God's supreme identity and authority. Together, these volumes form a complete testimony: the Supreme God is both exalted and near, both sovereign and personal.

May the revelations in these pages continue to strengthen your faith, steady your spirit, and remind you daily that the God who reveals His Name is faithful—and those who seek Him are never abandoned.

Encourage Others with Your Story

Your testimony carries power. If this *PrayerScripts* book has strengthened your faith, brought clarity to your spiritual life, or helped you experience breakthrough in any way, I invite you to share your experience by leaving a review on Amazon. Your words may be the very encouragement someone else needs to step into prayer, healing, deliverance, or deeper intimacy with God. Every review—short or long—helps others discover these resources and equips more believers to walk in victory. Thank you for taking a moment to share how God has used this book in your life.

More from PrayerScripts

THE SUPREME GOD (PART 1) SERIES

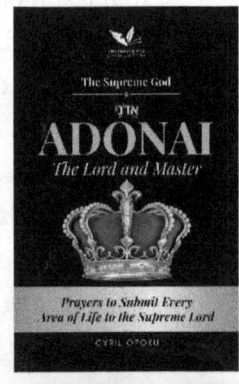

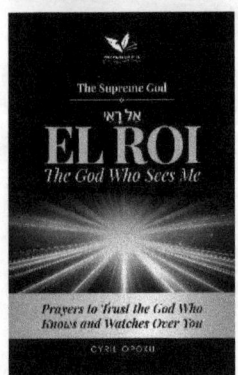

THE 7-14 REVIVAL PRAYERS SERIES

THIRST FOR GOD SERIES

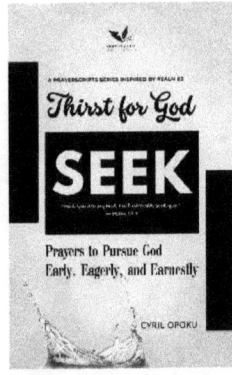
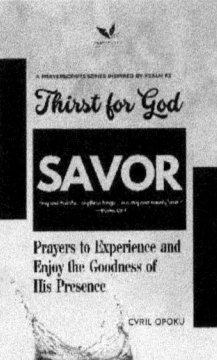

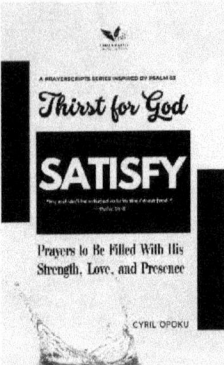

DEATH DEFEATED SERIES

"Brethren, Pray For Us" Series

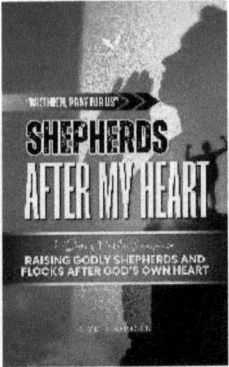

Demonic Dreams Destroyed Series

The Healing Covenant Series

Blueprints of Blessing Series

BLUEPRINTS OF BLESSING SERIES

THE PRAYER OF JABEZ SERIES

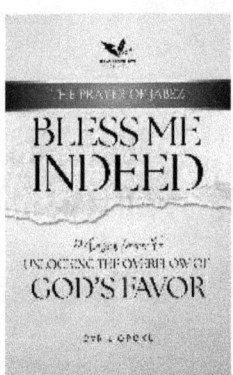
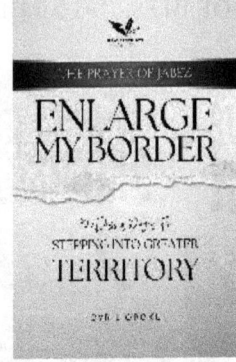

COMMAND YOUR DESTINY SERIES

COMMAND YOUR MORNING SERIES

COMMAND YOUR MORNING SERIES

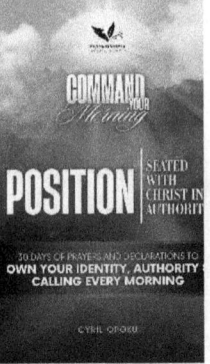

COMMAND YOUR NIGHT SERIES

EXPOSING THE ENEMY SERIES

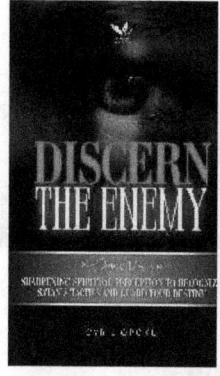

SPIRITUAL WARFARE SERIES

One Nation Under God Series

The Blood Covenant Series

www.ingramcontent.com/pod-product-compliance
Lightning Source LLC
Chambersburg PA
CBHW050552170426
43201CB00011B/1669